www.EffortlessMath.com

... So Much More Online!

✓ FREE Math lessons

✓ More Math learning books!

✓ Mathematics Worksheets

✓ Online Math Tutors

Need a PDF version of this book?

Please visit www.EffortlessMath.com

TSI Math Full Study Guide 2023 - 2024

Comprehensive Review + Practice Tests + Online Resources

By

Reza Nazari

Copyright © 2023

Effortless Math Education Inc.

All rights reserved. No part of this publication may be reproduced, stored in a retrieval system, or transmitted in any form or by any means, electronic, mechanical, photocopying, recording, scanning, or otherwise, except as permitted under Section 107 or 108 of the 1976 United States Copyright Ac, without permission of the author.

Effortless Math provides unofficial test prep products for a variety of tests and exams. It is not affiliated with or endorsed by any official organizations.

All inquiries should be addressed to:

info@effortlessMath.com

www.EffortlessMath.com

ISBN: 978-1-63719-100-2

Published by: Effortless Math Education Inc.

www.EffortlessMath.com

Visit www.EffortlessMath.com
for Online Math Practice

Welcome to
TSI Math Prep
2023

Thank you for choosing Effortless Math for your TSI Math test preparation and congratulations on making the decision to take the TSI test! It's a remarkable move you are taking, one that shouldn't be diminished in any capacity. That's why you need to use every tool possible to ensure you succeed on the test with the highest possible score, and this extensive study guide is one such tool.

If math has never been a strong subject for you, **don't worry**! This book will help you prepare for (and even ACE) the TSI test's math section. As test day draws nearer, effective preparation becomes increasingly more important. Thankfully, you have this comprehensive study guide to help you get ready for the test. With this guide, you can feel confident that you will be more than ready for the TSI Math test when the time comes.

First and foremost, it is important to note that this book is a study guide and not a textbook. It is best read from cover to cover. Every lesson of this "self-guided math book" was carefully developed to ensure that you are making the most effective use of your time while preparing for the test. This up-to-date guide reflects the 2023 test guidelines and will put you on the right track to hone your math skills, overcome exam anxiety, and boost your confidence, so that you do your best to succeed on the TSI Math test.

www.EffortlessMath.com

This study guide will:

☑ Explain the format of the TSI Math test.

☑ Describe specific test-taking strategies that you can use on the test.

☑ Provide TSI Math test-taking tips.

☑ Review all TSI Math concepts and topics you will be tested on.

☑ Help you identify the areas in which you need to concentrate your study time.

☑ Offer exercises that help you develop the basic math skills you will learn in each section.

☑ Give **2 realistic and full-length practice tests** (featuring new question types) with detailed answers to help you measure your exam readiness and build confidence.

This resource contains everything you will ever need to succeed on the TSI Math test. You'll get in-depth instructions on every math topic as well as tips and techniques on how to answer each question type. You'll also get plenty of practice questions to boost your test-taking confidence.

In addition, in the following pages you'll find:

➢ **How to Use This Book Effectively** – This section provides you with step-by-step instructions on how to get the most out of this comprehensive study guide.

➢ **How to study for the TSI Math Test** – A six-step study program has been developed to help you make the best use of this book and prepare for your TSI Math test. Here you'll find tips and strategies to guide your study program and help you understand TSI Math and how to ace the test.

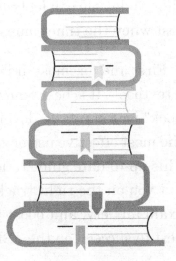

- ➢ **TSI Math Review** – Learn everything you need to know about the TSI Math test.

- ➢ **TSI Math Test-Taking Strategies** – Learn how to effectively put these recommended test-taking techniques into use for improving your TSI Math score.

- ➢ **Test Day Tips** – Review these tips to make sure you will do your best when the big day comes.

Effortless Math's TSI Online Center

Effortless Math Online TSI Center offers a complete study program, including the following:

- ✓ Step-by-step instructions on how to prepare for the TSI Math test
- ✓ Numerous TSI Math worksheets to help you measure your math skills
- ✓ Complete list of TSI Math formulas
- ✓ Video lessons for all TSI Math topics
- ✓ Full-length TSI Math practice tests
- ✓ And much more…

No Registration Required.

Visit **EffortlessMath.com/TSI** to find your online TSI Math resources.

How to Use This Book Effectively

Look no further when you need a study guide to improve your math skills to succeed on the math portion of the TSI test. Each chapter of this comprehensive guide to the TSI Math will provide you with the knowledge, tools, and understanding needed for every topic covered on the test.

It's imperative that you understand each topic before moving onto another one, as that's the way to guarantee your success. Each chapter provides you with examples and a step-by-step guide of every concept to better understand the content that will be on the test. To get the best possible results from this book:

> **Begin studying long before your test date.** This provides you ample time to learn the different math concepts. The earlier you begin studying for the test, the sharper your skills will be. Do not procrastinate! Provide yourself with plenty of time to learn the concepts and feel comfortable that you understand them when your test date arrives.

> **Practice consistently.** Study TSI Math concepts at least 20 to 30 minutes a day. Remember, slow and steady wins the race, which can be applied to preparing for the TSI Math test. Instead of cramming to tackle everything at once, be patient and learn the math topics in short bursts.
> Whenever you get a math problem wrong, **mark it off, and review it later** to make sure you understand the concept.
> Start each session by **looking over the previous material.**
> Once you've reviewed the book's lessons, **take the practice tests at the back of the book** to gauge your level of readiness. Then, review your results. Read detailed answers and solutions for each question you missed.
> **Take another practice test** to get an idea of how ready you are to take the actual exam. Taking the practice tests will give you the confidence you need on test day. Simulate the TSI testing environment by sitting in a quiet room free from distraction. Make sure to clock yourself with a timer.

How to Study for the TSI Math Test

Studying for the TSI Math test can be a really daunting and boring task. What's the best way to go about it? Is there a certain study method that works better than others? Well, studying for the TSI Math can be done effectively. The following six-step program has been designed to make preparing for the TSI Math test more efficient and less overwhelming.

Step 1 - Create a study plan
Step 2 - Choose your study resources
Step 3 - Review, Learn, Practice
Step 4 - Learn and practice test-taking strategies
Step 5 - Learn the TSI Test format and take practice tests
Step 6 - Analyze your performance

STEP 1: Create a Study Plan

It's always easier to get things done when you have a plan. Creating a study plan for the TSI Math test can help you to stay on track with your studies. It's important to sit down and prepare a study plan with what works with your life, work, and any other obligations you may have. Devote enough time each day to studying. It's also a great idea to break down each section of the exam into blocks and study one concept at a time.

It's important to understand that there is no "right" way to create a study plan. Your study plan will be personalized based on your specific needs and learning style. Follow these guidelines to create an effective study plan for your TSI Math test:

★ **Analyze your learning style and study habits** – Everyone has a different learning style. It is essential to embrace your individuality and the unique way you learn. Think about what works and what doesn't work for you. Do you prefer TSI Math prep books or a combination of textbooks and video lessons? Does it work better for you if you study every night for thirty minutes or is it more effective to study in the morning before going to work?

★ **Evaluate your schedule** – Review your current schedule and find out how much time you can consistently devote to TSI Math study.

★ **Develop a schedule** – Now it's time to add your study schedule to your calendar like any other obligation. Schedule time for study, practice, and review. Plan out which topic you will study on which day to ensure that you're devoting enough time to each concept. Develop a study plan that is mindful, realistic, and flexible.

★ **Stick to your schedule** – A study plan is only effective when it is followed consistently. You should try to develop a study plan that you can follow for the length of your study program.

★ **Evaluate your study plan and adjust as needed** – Sometimes you need to adjust your plan when you have new commitments. Check in with yourself regularly to make sure that you're not falling behind in your study plan. Remember, the most important thing is sticking to your plan. Your study plan is all about helping you be more productive. If you find that your study plan is not as effective as you want, don't get discouraged. It's okay to make changes as you figure out what works best for you.

STEP 2: Choose Your Study Resources

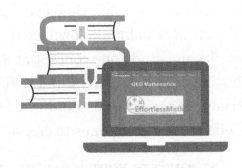

There are numerous textbooks and online resources available for the TSI Math test, and it may not be clear where to begin. Don't worry! This study guide provides everything you need to fully prepare for your TSI Math test. In addition to the book content, you can also use Effortless Math's online resources. (video lessons, worksheets, formulas, etc.) On each page, there is a link (and a QR code) to an online webpage which provides a comprehensive review of the topic, step-by-step instruction, video tutorial, and numerous examples and exercises to help you fully understand the concept.

You can also visit EffortlessMath.com/TSI to find your online TSI Math resources.

Step 3: Review, Learn, Practice

This TSI Math study guide breaks down each subject into specific skills or content areas. For instance, the percent concept is separated into different topics–percent calculation, percent increase and decrease, percent problems, etc. Use this study guide and Effortless Math online TSI center to help you go over all key math concepts and topics on the TSI Math test.

As you read each topic, take notes or highlight the concepts you would like to go over again in the future. If you're unfamiliar with a topic or something is difficult for you, use the link (or the QR code) at the bottom of the page to find the webpage that provides more instruction about that topic. For each math topic, plenty of instructions, step-by-step guides, and examples are provided to ensure you get a good grasp of the material.

Quickly review the topics you do understand to get a brush-up of the material. Be sure to do the practice questions provided at the end of every chapter to measure your understanding of the concepts.

Step 4: Learn and Practice Test-taking Strategies

In the following sections, you will find important test-taking strategies and tips that can help you earn extra points. You'll learn how to think strategically and when to guess if you don't know the answer to a question. Using TSI Math test-taking strategies and tips can help you raise your score and do well on the test. Apply test taking strategies on the practice tests to help you boost your confidence.

Step 5: Learn the TSI Test Format and Take Practice Tests

The *TSI Test Review* section provides information about the structure of the TSI test. Read this section to learn more about the TSI test structure, different test sections, the number of questions in each section, and the section time limits. When you have a prior understanding of the test format and different types of TSI Math questions, you'll feel more confident when you take the actual exam.

Once you have read through the instructions and lessons and feel like you are ready to go – take advantage of both of the full-length TSI Math practice tests available in this study guide. Use the practice tests to sharpen your skills and build confidence.

The TSI Math practice tests offered at the end of the book are formatted similarly to the actual TSI Math test. When you take each practice test, try to simulate actual testing conditions. To take the practice tests, sit in a quiet space, time yourself, and work through as many of the questions as time allows. The practice tests are followed by detailed answer explanations to help you find your weak areas, learn from your mistakes, and raise your TSI Math score.

Step 6: Analyze Your Performance

After taking the practice tests, look over the answer keys and explanations to learn which questions you answered correctly and which you did not. Never be discouraged if you make a few mistakes. See them as a learning opportunity. This will highlight your strengths and weaknesses.

You can use the results to determine if you need additional practice or if you are ready to take the actual TSI Math test.

Looking for more?

Visit EffortlessMath.com/TSI to find hundreds of TSI Math worksheets, video tutorials, practice tests, TSI Math formulas, and much more.

Or scan this QR code.

No Registration Required.

TSI Test Review

The Texas Success Initiative Assessment, is known as the TSI (or its new version TSIA2), is a test to determine the appropriate level of college course work for an incoming student. In essence, it is a broad and quick assessment of students' academic abilities.

The TSI test consists of three separate exams:

- Mathematics
- Reading
- Writing

The mathematics portion of the TSI test contains 20 questions. The test covers data analysis, geometry, and algebra on both intermediate and basic levels.

Students are not allowed to use calculator when taking a TSI assessment. A pop-up calculator is embedded in the test for some questions.

TSI Math Test-Taking Strategies

Here are some test-taking strategies that you can use to maximize your performance and results on the TSI Math test.

#1: Use This Approach To Answer Every TSI Math Question

- Review the question to identify keywords and important information.

- Translate the keywords into math operations so you can solve the problem.

- Review the answer choices. What are the differences between answer choices?

- Draw or label a diagram if needed.

- Try to find patterns.

- Find the right method to answer the question. Use straightforward math, plug in numbers, or test the answer choices (backsolving).

- Double-check your work.

#2: Use Educated Guessing

This approach is applicable to the problems you understand to some degree but cannot solve using straightforward math. In such cases, try to filter out as many answer choices as possible before picking an answer. In cases where you don't have a clue about what a certain problem entails, don't waste any time trying to eliminate answer choices. Just choose one randomly before moving onto the next question.

As you can ascertain, direct solutions are the most optimal approach. Carefully read through the question, determine what the solution is using the math you have learned before, then coordinate the answer with one of the choices available to you. Are you stumped? Make your best guess, then move on.

Don't leave any fields empty! Even if you're unable to work out a problem, strive to answer it. Take a guess if you have to. You will not lose points by getting an answer wrong, though you may gain a point by getting it correct!

#3: BALLPARK

A ballpark answer is a rough approximation. When we become overwhelmed by calculations and figures, we end up making silly mistakes. A decimal that is moved by one unit can change an answer from right to wrong, regardless of the number of steps that you went through to get it. That's where ballparking can play a big part.

If you think you know what the correct answer may be (even if it's just a ballpark answer), you'll usually have the ability to eliminate a couple of choices. While answer choices are usually based on the average student error and/or values that are closely tied, you will still be able to weed out choices that are way far afield. Try to find answers that aren't in the proverbial ballpark when you're looking for a wrong answer on a multiple-choice question. This is an optimal approach to eliminating answers to a problem.

#4: BACKSOLVING

All questions on the TSI Math test will be in multiple-choice format. Many test-takers prefer multiple-choice questions, as at least the answer is right there. You'll typically have four answers to pick from. You simply need to figure out which one is correct. Usually, the best way to go about doing so is "backsolving."

As mentioned earlier, direct solutions are the most optimal approach to answering a question. Carefully read through a problem, calculate a solution, then correspond the answer with one of the choices displayed in front of you. If you can't calculate a solution, your next best approach involves "backsolving."

When backsolving a problem, contrast one of your answer options against the problem you are asked, then see which of them is most relevant. More often than not, answer choices are listed in ascending or descending order. In such cases, try out the choices B or C. If it's not correct, you can go either down or up from there.

#5 : Plugging In Numbers

"Plugging in numbers" is a strategy that can be applied to a wide range of different math problems on the TSI Math test. This approach is typically used to simplify a challenging question so that it is more understandable. By using the strategy carefully, you can find the answer without too much trouble.

The concept is fairly straightforward–replace unknown variables in a problem with certain values. When selecting a number, consider the following:

- Choose a number that's basic (just not too basic). Generally, you should avoid choosing 1 (or even 0). A decent choice is 2.

- Try not to choose a number that is displayed in the problem.

- Make sure you keep your numbers different if you need to choose at least two of them.

- More often than not, choosing numbers merely lets you filter out some of your answer choices. As such, don't just go with the first choice that gives you the right answer.

- If several answers seem correct, then you'll need to choose another value and try again. This time, though, you'll just need to check choices that haven't been eliminated yet.

- If your question contains fractions, then a potential right answer may involve either an LCD (least common denominator) or an LCD multiple.

- 100 is the number you should choose when you are dealing with problems involving percentages.

TSI Mathematics – Test Day Tips

After practicing and reviewing all the math concepts you've been taught, and taking some TSI mathematics practice tests, you'll be prepared for test day. Consider the following tips to be extra-ready come test time.

Before Your Test

What to do the night before:

- **Relax!** One day before your test, study lightly or skip studying altogether. You shouldn't attempt to learn something new, either. There are plenty of reasons why studying the evening before a big test can work against you. Put it this way—a marathoner wouldn't go out for a sprint before the day of a big race. Mental marathoners—such as yourself—should not study for any more than one hour 24 hours before a TSI test. That's because your brain requires some rest to be at its best. The night before your exam, spend some time with family or friends, or read a book.

- **Avoid bright screens** - You'll have to get some good shuteye the night before your test. Bright screens (such as the ones coming from your laptop, TV, or mobile device) should be avoided altogether. Staring at such a screen will keep your brain up, making it hard to drift asleep at a reasonable hour.

- **Make sure your dinner is healthy** - The meal that you have for dinner should be nutritious. Be sure to drink plenty of water as well. Load up on your complex carbohydrates, much like a marathon runner would do. Pasta, rice, and potatoes are ideal options here, as are vegetables and protein sources.

- **Get your bag ready for test day** - The night prior to your test, pack your bag with your stationery, admissions pass, ID, and any other gear that you need. Keep the bag right by your front door.

- **Make plans to reach the testing site** - Before going to sleep, ensure that you understand precisely how you will arrive at the site of the test. If parking is something you'll have to find first, plan for it. If you're dependent on public transit, then review the schedule. You should also make sure that the train/bus/subway/streetcar you use will be running. Find out about road closures as well. If a parent or friend is accompanying you, ensure that they understand what steps they have to take as well.

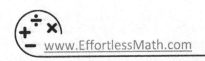

The Day of the Test

- **Get up reasonably early, but not too early.**

- **Have breakfast** - Breakfast improves your concentration, memory, and mood. As such, make sure the breakfast that you eat in the morning is healthy. The last thing you want to be is distracted by a grumbling tummy. If it's not your own stomach making those noises, another test taker close to you might be instead. Prevent discomfort or embarrassment by consuming a healthy breakfast. Bring a snack with you if you think you'll need it.

- **Follow your daily routine** - Do you watch Good Morning America each morning while getting ready for the day? Don't break your usual habits on the day of the test. Likewise, if coffee isn't something you drink in the morning, then don't take up the habit hours before your test. Routine consistency lets you concentrate on the main objective—doing the best you can on your test.

- **Wear layers** - Dress yourself up in comfortable layers. You should be ready for any kind of internal temperature. If it gets too warm during the test, take a layer off.

- **Get there on time** - The last thing you want to do is get to the test site late. Rather, you should be there 45 minutes prior to the start of the test. Upon your arrival, try not to hang out with anybody who is nervous. Any anxious energy they exhibit shouldn't influence you.

- **Leave the books at home** - No books should be brought to the test site. If you start developing anxiety before the test, books could encourage you to do some last-minute studying, which will only hinder you. Keep the books far away—better yet, leave them at home.

- **Make your voice heard** - If something is off, speak to a proctor. If medical attention is needed or if you'll require anything, consult the proctor prior to the start of the test. Any doubts you have should be clarified. You should be entering the test site with a state of mind that is completely clear.

- **Have faith in yourself** - When you feel confident, you will be able to perform at your best. When you are waiting for the test to begin, envision yourself receiving an outstanding result. Try to see yourself as someone who knows all the answers, no matter what the questions are. A lot of athletes tend to use this technique–particularly before a big competition. Your expectations will be reflected by your performance.

During your test

- **Be calm and breathe deeply** - You need to relax before the test, and some deep breathing will go a long way to help you do that. Be confident and calm. You got this. Everybody feels a little stressed out just before an evaluation of any kind is set to begin. Learn some effective breathing exercises. Spend a minute meditating before the test starts. Filter out any negative thoughts you have. Exhibit confidence when having such thoughts.

- **Concentrate on the test** - Refrain from comparing yourself to anyone else. You shouldn't be distracted by the people near you or random noise. Concentrate exclusively on the test. If you find yourself irritated by surrounding noises, earplugs can be used to block sounds off close to you. Don't forget–the test is going to last several hours if you're taking more than one subject of the test. Some of that time will be dedicated to brief sections. Concentrate on the specific section you are working on during a particular moment. Do not let your mind wander off to upcoming or previous sections.

- **Try to answer each question individually** - Focus only on the question you are working on. Use one of the test-taking strategies to solve the problem. If you aren't able to come up with an answer, don't get frustrated. Simply skip that question, then move onto the next one.

- **Don't forget to breathe!** Whenever you notice your mind wandering, your stress levels boosting, or frustration brewing, take a thirty-second break. Shut your eyes, drop your pencil, breathe deeply, and let your shoulders relax. You will end up being more productive when you allow yourself to relax for a moment.

- **Optimize your breaks** - When break time comes, use the restroom, have a snack, and reactivate your energy for the subsequent section. Doing some stretches can help stimulate your blood flow.

After your test

- **Take it easy** - You will need to set some time aside to relax and decompress once the test has concluded. There is no need to stress yourself out about what you could've said, or what you may have done wrong. At this point, there's nothing you can do about it. Your energy and time would be better spent on something that will bring you happiness for the remainder of your day.

- **Redoing the test** - Did you pass the test? Congratulations! Your hard work paid off!

If you have failed your test, though, don't worry! The test can be retaken. In such cases, you will need to follow the retake policy. You also need to re-register to take the exam again.

Contents

Chapter 1
- Fractions and Mixed Numbers 1
- Simplifying Fractions 2
- Adding and Subtracting Fractions 3
- Multiplying and Dividing Fractions 4
- Adding Mixed Numbers 5
- Subtracting Mixed Numbers 6
- Multiplying Mixed Numbers 7
- Dividing Mixed Numbers 8
- Chapter 1: Answers 9

Chapter 2
- Decimals 11
- Comparing Decimals 12
- Rounding Decimals 13
- Adding and Subtracting Decimals 14
- Multiplying and Dividing Decimals 15
- Chapter 2: Answers 16

Chapter 3
- Integers and Order of Operations 17
- Adding and Subtracting Integers 18
- Multiplying and Dividing Integers 19
- Order of Operation 20
- Integers and Absolute Value 21
- Chapter 3: Answers 22

Chapter 4
- Ratios and Proportions 23
- Simplifying Ratios 24
- Proportional Ratios 25
- Create Proportion 26
- Similarity and Ratios 27
- Chapter 4: Answers 28

www.EffortlessMath.com

Chapter 5

- Percentage 29
- Percent Problems 30
- Percent of Increase and Decrease 31
- Discount, Tax and Tip 32
- Simple Interest 33
- Chapter 5: Answers 34

Chapter 6

- Expressions and Variables 35
- Simplifying Variable Expressions 36
- Simplifying Polynomial Expressions 37
- Evaluating One Variable 38
- Evaluating Two Variables 39
- The Distributive Property 40
- Chapter 6: Answers 42

Chapter 7

- Equations and Inequalities 43
- One–Step Equations 44
- Multi –Step Equations 45
- System of Equations 46
- Graphing Single–Variable Inequalities 47
- One–Step Inequalities 48
- Multi – Step Inequalities 49
- Chapter 7: Answers 50

Chapter 8

- Lines and Slope 53
- Finding Slope 54
- Graphing Lines Using Slope–Intercept Form 55
- Writing Linear Equations 56
- Finding Midpoint 57
- Finding Distance of Two Points 58
- Chapter 8: Answers 60

Chapter 9: Exponents and Variables ... 61

- Multiplication Property of Exponents ... 62
- Division Property of Exponents ... 63
- Powers of Products and Quotients ... 64
- Zero and Negative Exponents ... 65
- Negative Exponents and Negative Bases ... 66
- Scientific Notation ... 67
- Radicals ... 68
- Chapter 9: Answers ... 69

Chapter 10: Polynomials ... 71

- Simplifying Polynomials ... 72
- Adding and Subtracting Polynomials ... 73
- Multiplying Binomials ... 74
- Multiplying and Dividing Monomials ... 75
- Multiplying a Polynomial and a Monomial ... 76
- Multiplying Monomials ... 77
- Factoring Trinomials ... 78
- Chapter 10: Answers ... 79

Chapter 11: Geometry and Solid Figures ... 81

- The Pythagorean Theorem ... 82
- Complementary and Supplementary Angles ... 83
- Parallel lines and Transversals ... 84
- Triangles ... 85
- Special Right Triangles ... 86
- Polygons ... 87
- Circles ... 88
- Cubes ... 89
- Trapezoids ... 90
- Rectangular Prisms ... 91
- Cylinder ... 92
- Chapter 11: Answers ... 93

Chapter 12: Statistics ... 95

- Mean, Median, Mode, and Range of the Given Data ... 96
- Probability Problems ... 97
- Pie Graph ... 98
- Permutations and Combinations ... 99
- Chapter 12: Answers ... 100

Chapter 13: Functions Operations ... 101

- Function Notation and Evaluation ... 102
- Adding and Subtracting Functions ... 103
- Multiplying and Dividing Functions ... 104
- Composition of Functions ... 105
- Chapter 13: Answers ... 106

Time to Test ... 107
TSI Mathematics Practice Test 1 ... 109
TSI Mathematics Practice Test 2 ... 117
TSI Mathematics Practice Test Answers ... 126
TSI Mathematics Practice Test Answers and Explanations ... 127

CHAPTER 1
Fractions and Mixed Numbers

Math topics that you'll learn in this chapter:

- ✓ Simplifying Fractions
- ✓ Adding and Subtracting Fractions
- ✓ Multiplying and Dividing Fractions
- ✓ Adding Mixed Numbers
- ✓ Subtracting Mixed Numbers
- ✓ Multiplying Mixed Numbers
- ✓ Dividing Mixed Numbers

Fractions and Mixed Numbers

Topic	Simplifying Fractions
Notes	✓ Evenly divide both the top and bottom of the fraction by 2, 3, 5, 7, ... etc. ✓ Continue until you can't go any further.
Example	**Simplify** $\frac{72}{96}$ To simplify $\frac{72}{96}$, find a number that both 72 and 96 are divisible by. Both are divisible by 24. Then: $\frac{72}{96} = \frac{72 \div 24}{96 \div 24} = \frac{3}{4}$
Your Turn!	1) $\frac{4}{12} =$	2) $\frac{11}{44} =$
	3) $\frac{13}{39} =$	4) $\frac{12}{48} =$
	5) $\frac{14}{63} =$	6) $\frac{20}{120} =$
	7) $\frac{27}{72} =$	8) $\frac{36}{96} =$
	9) $\frac{35}{65} =$	10) $\frac{36}{88} =$

Topic	Adding and Subtracting Fractions
Notes	- For "like" fractions (fractions with the same denominator), add or subtract the numerators and write the answer over the common denominator. - Find equivalent fractions with the same denominator before you can add or subtract fractions with different denominators. - Adding and Subtracting with the same denominator: $$\frac{a}{b}+\frac{c}{b}=\frac{a+c}{b}, \frac{a}{b}-\frac{c}{b}=\frac{a-c}{b}$$ - Adding and Subtracting fractions with different denominators: $$\frac{a}{b}+\frac{c}{d}=\frac{ad+bc}{bd}, \frac{a}{b}-\frac{c}{d}=\frac{ad-bc}{bd}$$
Example	**Find the sum.** $\frac{1}{3}+\frac{2}{5}=$ For "unlike" fractions, find equivalent fractions with the same denominator before you can add fractions with different denominators. Use this formula: $\frac{a}{b}+\frac{c}{b}=\frac{a+c}{b} \rightarrow \frac{(5)(1)+(3)(2)}{3\times 5}=\frac{11}{15}$ **Subtract.** $\frac{6}{5}-\frac{3}{5}$ For like fractions, subtract and write the answer over the common denominator: $\frac{6-3}{5}=\frac{3}{5}$
Your Turn!	1) $\frac{2}{7}+\frac{3}{7}=$ 2) $\frac{7}{8}-\frac{1}{4}=$
	3) $\frac{4}{5}+\frac{1}{9}=$ 4) $\frac{3}{7}-\frac{1}{4}=$
Find more at bit.ly/3nKet2X	5) $\frac{2}{9}+\frac{3}{4}=$ 6) $\frac{5}{6}-\frac{2}{5}=$
	7) $\frac{1}{3}+\frac{3}{8}=$ 8) $\frac{9}{11}-\frac{2}{3}=$

Fractions and Mixed Numbers

Multiplying and Dividing Fractions

Topic	
Notes	✓ Multiplying fractions: multiply the top numbers and multiply the bottom numbers. ✓ Dividing fractions: Keep, Change, Flip Keep first fraction, change division sign to multiplication, and flip the numerator and denominator of the second fraction. Then, solve!
Examples	**Multiply.** $\frac{2}{7} \times \frac{1}{6} =$ Multiply the top numbers and multiply the bottom numbers. $\frac{2}{7} \times \frac{1}{6} = \frac{2 \times 1}{7 \times 6} = \frac{2}{42}$, simplify: $\frac{2}{42} = \frac{2 \div 2}{42 \div 2} = \frac{1}{21}$ **Divide.** $\frac{2}{6} \div \frac{2}{3} =$ Keep first fraction, change division sign to multiplication, and flip the numerator and denominator of the second fraction. Then: $\frac{2}{6} \div \frac{2}{3} = \frac{2}{6} \times \frac{3}{2} = \frac{2 \times 3}{6 \times 2} = \frac{6 \div 6}{12 \div 6} = \frac{1}{2}$
Your Turn!	1) $\frac{3}{4} \times \frac{2}{3} =$ 2) $\frac{3}{8} \div \frac{2}{3} =$
	3) $\frac{3}{8} \times \frac{4}{5} =$ 4) $\frac{4}{5} \div \frac{4}{15} =$
	5) $\frac{1}{8} \times \frac{3}{7} =$ 6) $\frac{5}{9} \div \frac{4}{7} =$
	7) $\frac{2}{15} \times \frac{3}{8} =$ 8) $\frac{1}{9} \div \frac{5}{6} =$

Find more at
bit.ly/3haSiQW

Topic	Adding Mixed Numbers
Notes	Use the following steps for adding mixed numbers. ✓ Add whole numbers of the mixed numbers. ✓ Add the fractions of each mixed number. ✓ Find the Least Common Denominator (LCD) if necessary. ✓ Add whole numbers and fractions. ✓ Write your answer in lowest terms.
Example	**Add mixed numbers.** $1\frac{1}{2} + 2\frac{2}{3} =$ Rewriting our equation with parts separated, $1 + \frac{1}{2} + 2 + \frac{2}{3}$ Add whole numbers: $1 + 2 = 3$ Add fractions: $\frac{1}{2} + \frac{2}{3} = \frac{3}{6} + \frac{4}{6} = \frac{7}{6} = 1\frac{1}{6}$, Now, combine the whole and fraction parts: $3 + 1 + \frac{1}{6} = 4\frac{1}{6}$

Your Turn!

1) $9\frac{1}{2} + 5\frac{3}{4} =$

2) $4\frac{3}{2} + 2\frac{1}{6} =$

3) $6\frac{3}{4} + 3\frac{5}{28} =$

4) $4\frac{2}{5} + 6\frac{2}{4} =$

5) $4\frac{6}{7} + 5\frac{3}{5} =$

6) $3\frac{1}{6} + 1\frac{2}{7} =$

7) $4\frac{5}{9} + 2\frac{2}{7} =$

8) $7\frac{1}{9} + 5\frac{2}{6} =$

Find more at
bit.ly/2M4oABB

Fractions and Mixed Numbers

Topic	Subtracting Mixed Numbers
Notes	Use the following steps for subtracting mixed numbers. ✓ Convert mixed numbers into improper fractions. $a\frac{c}{b} = \frac{ab+c}{b}$ ✓ Find equivalent fractions with the same denominator for unlike fractions (fractions with different denominators) ✓ Subtract the second fraction from the first one. ✓ Write your answer in lowest terms and convert it into a mixed number if the answer is an improper fraction.
Example	**Subtract.** $9\frac{1}{2} - 5\frac{1}{4} =$ Convert mixed numbers into fractions: $9\frac{1}{2} = \frac{9\times 2+1}{2} = \frac{19}{2}$ and $5\frac{1}{4} = \frac{5\times 4+1}{4} = \frac{21}{4}$, these two fractions are "unlike" fractions. (they have different denominators). Find equivalent fractions with the same denominator. Use this formula: $\frac{a}{b} - \frac{c}{d} = \frac{ad-bc}{bd}$ $\frac{19}{2} - \frac{21}{4} = \frac{(19)(4)-(21)(2)}{2\times 4} = \frac{76-42}{8} = \frac{34}{8}$, the answer is an improper fraction, convert it into a mixed number. $\frac{34}{8} = 4\frac{2}{8} = 4\frac{1}{4}$
Your Turn!	1) $3\frac{3}{4} - 1\frac{1}{2} =$ 2) $2\frac{4}{9} - 1\frac{2}{3} =$
	3) $5\frac{1}{6} - 2\frac{5}{12} =$ 4) $5\frac{1}{3} - 1\frac{3}{4} =$
	5) $4\frac{5}{6} - 1\frac{1}{8} =$ 6) $7\frac{3}{4} - 1\frac{2}{3} =$
	7) $9\frac{5}{6} - 5\frac{1}{5} =$ 8) $4\frac{1}{4} - 3\frac{7}{9} =$

Find more at
bit.ly/3aD3KDG

Topic	Multiplying Mixed Numbers
Notes	✓ Convert the mixed numbers into fractions. $a\frac{c}{b} = a + \frac{c}{b} = \frac{ab+c}{b}$ ✓ Multiply fractions and simplify if necessary. $\frac{a}{b} \times \frac{c}{d} = \frac{a \times c}{b \times d}$ ✓ If the answer is an improper fraction (numerator is bigger than denominator), convert it into a mixed number.
Example	**Multiply** $2\frac{1}{2} \times 4\frac{1}{3}$ Convert mixed numbers into fractions: $2\frac{1}{2} = \frac{2 \times 2 + 1}{2} = \frac{5}{2}$ and $4\frac{1}{3} = \frac{4 \times 3 + 1}{3} = \frac{13}{3}$ Multiply two fractions: $\frac{5}{2} \times \frac{13}{3} = \frac{5 \times 13}{2 \times 3} = \frac{65}{6}$ The answer is an improper fraction. Convert it into a mixed number: $$\frac{65}{6} = 10\frac{5}{6}$$
Your Turn!	1) $2\frac{2}{3} \times 1\frac{2}{3} =$ 2) $4\frac{1}{5} \times 2\frac{2}{3} =$ 3) $3\frac{3}{5} \times 3\frac{2}{3} =$ 4) $3\frac{1}{2} \times 4\frac{1}{3} =$ 5) $5\frac{3}{4} \times 2\frac{1}{5} =$ 6) $6\frac{3}{7} \times 9\frac{1}{4} =$ 7) $4\frac{4}{5} \times 3\frac{2}{3} =$ 8) $5\frac{1}{6} \times 3\frac{1}{4} =$

Find more at

bit.ly/3aPy7XJ

Topic	Dividing Mixed Numbers
Notes	✓ Convert the mixed numbers into improper fractions. $$a\frac{c}{b} = a + \frac{c}{b} = \frac{ab+c}{b}$$ ✓ Divide fractions and simplify if necessary.
Example	**Solve.** $1\frac{1}{2} \div 3\frac{1}{8} =$ Converting mixed numbers to fractions: $1\frac{1}{2} \div 3\frac{1}{8} = \frac{3}{2} \div \frac{25}{8}$ Keep, Change, Flip: $\frac{3}{2} \div \frac{25}{8} = \frac{3}{2} \times \frac{8}{25} = \frac{3 \times 8}{2 \times 25} = \frac{24}{50} = \frac{12}{25}$
Your Turn!	1) $6\frac{1}{2} \div 2\frac{1}{4} =$ 2) $3\frac{1}{3} \div 2\frac{3}{5} =$ 3) $2\frac{3}{4} \div 1\frac{1}{2} =$ 4) $6\frac{2}{3} \div 4\frac{3}{4} =$ 5) $1\frac{1}{3} \div 8\frac{2}{3} =$ 6) $8\frac{1}{4} \div 4\frac{1}{2} =$ 7) $2\frac{4}{5} \div 3\frac{2}{9} =$ 8) $8\frac{3}{4} \div 2\frac{5}{8} =$ 9) $4\frac{1}{6} \div 2\frac{5}{3} =$ 10) $4\frac{3}{8} \div 4\frac{1}{4} =$

Find more at

bit.ly/2KLPk9k

Chapter 1: Answers

Simplifying Fractions

1) $\frac{1}{3}$
2) $\frac{1}{4}$
3) $\frac{1}{3}$
4) $\frac{1}{4}$
5) $\frac{2}{9}$
6) $\frac{1}{6}$
7) $\frac{3}{8}$
8) $\frac{3}{8}$
9) $\frac{7}{13}$
10) $\frac{9}{22}$

Adding and Subtracting Fractions

1) $\frac{5}{7}$
2) $\frac{5}{8}$
3) $\frac{41}{45}$
4) $\frac{5}{28}$
5) $\frac{35}{36}$
6) $\frac{13}{30}$
7) $\frac{17}{24}$
8) $\frac{5}{33}$

Multiplying and Dividing Fractions

1) $\frac{1}{2}$
2) $\frac{9}{16}$
3) $\frac{3}{10}$
4) 3
5) $\frac{3}{56}$
6) $\frac{35}{36}$
7) $\frac{1}{20}$
8) $\frac{2}{15}$

Adding Mixed Numbers

1) $15\frac{1}{4}$
2) $7\frac{2}{3}$
3) $9\frac{13}{14}$
4) $10\frac{9}{10}$
5) $10\frac{16}{35}$
6) $4\frac{19}{42}$
7) $6\frac{53}{63}$
8) $12\frac{4}{9}$

Fractions and Mixed Numbers

Subtracting Mixed Numbers

1) $2\frac{1}{4}$
2) $\frac{7}{9}$
3) $2\frac{3}{4}$
4) $3\frac{7}{12}$
5) $3\frac{17}{24}$
6) $6\frac{1}{12}$
7) $4\frac{19}{30}$
8) $\frac{17}{36}$

Multiplying Mixed Numbers

1) $4\frac{4}{9}$
2) $11\frac{1}{5}$
3) $13\frac{1}{5}$
4) $15\frac{1}{16}$
5) $12\frac{13}{20}$
6) $59\frac{13}{28}$
7) $17\frac{3}{5}$
8) $16\frac{19}{24}$

Dividing Mixed Numbers

1) $2\frac{8}{9}$
2) $1\frac{11}{39}$
3) $1\frac{5}{6}$
4) $1\frac{23}{57}$
5) $\frac{2}{13}$
6) $1\frac{5}{6}$
7) $\frac{126}{145}$
8) $3\frac{1}{3}$
9) $1\frac{3}{22}$
10) $1\frac{1}{34}$

CHAPTER 2: Decimals

Math topics that you'll learn in this chapter:

- ✓ Comparing Decimals
- ✓ Rounding Decimals
- ✓ Adding and Subtracting Decimals
- ✓ Multiplying and Dividing Decimals

Topic	Comparing Decimals
Notes	Decimals: is a fraction written in a special form. For example, instead of writing $\frac{1}{2}$ you can write **0.5**. For comparing decimals: ✓ Compare each digit of two decimals in the same place value. ✓ Start from left. Compare hundreds, tens, ones, tenth, hundredth, etc. ✓ To compare numbers, use these symbols: - Equal to =, Less than <, Greater than > Greater than or equal ≥, Less than or equal ≤
Examples	*Compare* **0.60** *and* **0.06**. 0.60 is greater than 0.06, because the tenth place of 0.60 is 6, but the tenth place of 0.06 is zero. Then: $0.60 > 0.06$ *Compare* **0.0751** *and* **0.751**. 0.751 is greater than 0.0751, because the tenth place of 0.751 is 7, but the tenth place of 0.0751 is zero. Then: $0.0751 < 0.751$

Your Turn!		
	1) 0.44 ☐ 0.48	2) 1.23 ☐ 1.30
	3) 15.55 ☐ 18.08	4) 2.57 ☐ 2.058
	5) 1.356 ☐ 13.56	6) 0.73 ☐ 0.730
	7) 3.689 ☐ 3.698	8) 0.652 ☐ 0.625

Find more at

bit.ly/2WHt2Za

Topic	**Rounding Decimals**
Notes	✓ We can round decimals to a certain accuracy or number of decimal places. ✓ Let's review place values: For example: $$35.4817$$ 3: tens 5: ones 4: tenths 8: hundredths 1: thousandths 7: tens thousandths ✓ To round a decimal, find the place value you'll round to. ✓ Find the digit to the right of the place value you're rounding to. If it is 5 or bigger, add 1 to the place value you're rounding to and remove all digits on its right side. If the digit to the right of the place value is less than 5, keep the place value and remove all digits on the right.
Example	**Round 11.7268 to the hundredth-place value.** First look at the next place value to the right, (thousandths). It's 6 and it is greater than 5. Thus add 1 to the digit in the hundredth place. It is 2. → $2 + 1 = 3$, then, the answer is 11.73
Your Turn!	*Round each number to the underlined place value.*

1) 22.5<u>6</u>6 =	2) 1.3<u>2</u>5 =
3) 52.<u>4</u>26 =	4) 3<u>5</u>.72 =
5) 10.<u>2</u>59 =	6) 32.5<u>0</u>6 =
7) 6.4<u>8</u>1 =	8) 8.0<u>1</u>9 =

Find more at

bit.ly/3mKEluf

Adding and Subtracting Decimals

Notes
- ✓ Line up the numbers.
- ✓ Add zeros to have same number of digits for both numbers if necessary.
- ✓ Add or subtract using column addition or subtraction.

Examples

Add. $3.8 + 5.14 =$

First line up the numbers: $\begin{array}{r}3.8\\+5.14\\\hline\end{array}$ →Add zeros to have same number of digits for both numbers. $\begin{array}{r}3.80\\+5.14\\\hline\end{array}$ → Start with the hundredths place. $0 + 4 = 4$, $\begin{array}{r}3.80\\+5.14\\\hline 4\end{array}$ → Continue with tenths place. $8 + 1 = 9$, $\begin{array}{r}3.80\\+5.14\\\hline .94\end{array}$ → Add the ones place. $3 + 5 = 8$, $\begin{array}{r}3.80\\+5.14\\\hline 8.94\end{array}$

Subtract. $6.56 - 4.13 = \begin{array}{r}6.56\\-4.13\\\hline\end{array}$

Start with the hundredths place. $6 - 3 = 3$, $\begin{array}{r}6.56\\-4.13\\\hline 3\end{array}$, continue with tenths place. $5 - 1 = 4$, $\begin{array}{r}6.56\\-4.13\\\hline .43\end{array}$, subtract the ones place. $6 - 4 = 2$, $\begin{array}{r}6.56\\-4.13\\\hline 2.43\end{array}$

Your Turn!

1) $26.20 + 11.55 =$

2) $62.25 - 26.10 =$

3) $39.61 + 26.12 =$

4) $55.58 - 42.26 =$

5) $29.23 + 33.58 =$

6) $33.48 - 24.40 =$

Find more at
bit.ly/38uyUdx

Topic	Multiplying and Dividing Decimals
Notes	For Multiplication: ✓ Ignore the decimal point and set up and multiply the numbers as you do with whole numbers. ✓ Count the total number of decimal places in both factors. ✓ Place the decimal point in the product. For Division: ✓ If the divisor is not a whole number, move decimal point to right to make it a whole number. Do the same for dividend. ✓ Divide similar to whole numbers.
Examples	**Find the product.** $1.4 \times 2.6 =$ Set up and multiply the numbers as you do with whole numbers. Line up the numbers: $\frac{14}{\times 26}$ → Multiply: $\frac{14}{\times 26}\over{364}$ → Count the total number of decimal places in both of the factors. There are two decimal digits. Then: $1.4 \times 2.6 = 3.64$ **Find the quotient.** $4.8 \div 0.6 =$ The divisor is not a whole number. Multiply it by 10 to get 6. → $0.6 \times 10 = 6$ Do the same for the dividend to get 48 → $4.8 \times 10 = 48$ Now, divide: $48 \div 6 = 8$. The answer is 8.
Your Turn! Find more at bit.ly/34DZ0cS	1) $1.24 \times 0.2 =$ 2) $56.8 \div 0.2 =$ 3) $0.8 \times 0.42 =$ 4) $36.6 \div 0.6 =$ 5) $0.25 \times 0.5 =$ 6) $26.8 \div 100 =$

Chapter 2: Answers

Comparing Decimals

1) <
2) <
3) <
4) >
5) <
6) =
7) <
8) >

Rounding Decimals

1) 22.57
2) 1.33
3) 52.4
4) 40
5) 10.3
6) 32.51
7) 6.48
8) 8.02

Adding and Subtracting Decimals

1) 37.75
2) 36.15
3) 65.73
4) 13.32
5) 62.81
6) 9.08

Multiplying and Dividing Decimals

1) 0.248
2) 284
3) 0.336
4) 61
5) 0.125
6) 0.268

CHAPTER 3
Integers and Order of Operations

Math topics that you'll learn in this chapter:

- ✓ Adding and Subtracting Integers
- ✓ Multiplying and Dividing Integers
- ✓ Order of Operations
- ✓ Integers and Absolute Value

Integers and Order of Operations

Topic	Adding and Subtracting Integers
Notes	✓ Integers include: zero, counting numbers, and the negative of the counting numbers. $\{\ldots, -3, -2, -1, 0, 1, 2, 3, \ldots\}$ ✓ Add a positive integer by moving to the right on the number line. ✓ Add a negative integer by moving to the left on the number line. Subtract an integer by adding its opposite.
Examples	**Solve.** $(5) - (-3) =$ Keep the first number and convert the sign of the second number to its opposite. (change subtraction into addition. Then: $(5) + 3 = 8$ **Solve.** $48 + (20 - 34) =$ First subtract the numbers in brackets, $20 - 34 = -14$ Then: $48 + (-14) = \rightarrow$ change addition into subtraction: $48 - 14 = 34$

Your Turn!

1) $-(15) + 10 =$	2) $(-9) + (-12) =$
3) $-(-16) + 3 =$	4) $5 - (-2) + 11 =$
5) $(-4) + (-6) + 2 =$	6) $19 - (-2 + 6) =$
7) $-7 + (-14) + 9 =$	8) $-(20) - (-3) + 8 =$

Find more at bit.ly/3aKx5vl

Topic	**Multiplying and Dividing Integers**
Notes	Use following rules for multiplying and dividing integers: ✓ (negative) × (negative) = positive ✓ (negative) ÷ (negative) = positive ✓ (negative) × (positive) = negative ✓ (negative) ÷ (positive) = negative ✓ (positive) × (positive) = positive ✓ (positive) ÷ (negative) = negative
Examples	**Solve.** $6 \times (11 - 5) =$ First subtract the numbers in brackets, $11 - 5 = 6 \rightarrow (6) \times (6) =$ Now use this rule: (positive) × (positive) = positive $(6) \times (6) = 36$ **Solve.** $(-36) + (-25 \div 5) =$ First divide -25 by 5, the numbers in brackets, using this rule: (negative) ÷ (positive) = negative Then: $-25 \div 5 = -5$. Now, add -36 and -5: $(-36) + (-5) = -36 - 5 = -41$
Your Turn!	1) $(-7) \times 3 =$ 2) $(-56) \div (8) =$
	3) $(-14) \times (-4) =$ 4) $-63 \div (-9) =$
Find more at bit.ly/3pjQW98	5) $(18 - 11) \times (-6) =$ 6) $(-15) \div (3 - 6) =$
	7) $8 \times (-7 + 6) =$ 8) $(24) \div (-3 - 5) =$

Integers and Order of Operations

Topic	Order of Operation
Notes	When there is more than one math operation, use PEMDAS: (to memorize this rule, remember the phrase "Please Excuse My Dear Aunt Sally") ✓ Parentheses ✓ Exponents ✓ Multiplication and Division (from left to right) ✓ Addition and Subtraction (from left to right)
Examples	**Calculate.** $(18 - 26) \div (2^3 \div 4) =$ First simplify inside parentheses: $(-8) \div (8 \div 4) = (-8) \div (2)$ Then: $(-8) \div (2) = -4$ **Solve.** $(-6 \times 7) - (14 - 3^2) =$ First calculate within parentheses: $(-6 \times 7) - (14 - 3^2) = (-42) - (14 - 9)$ Then: $(-42) - (14 - 9) = -42 - 5 = -47$

Your Turn!

1) $(11 \times 3) \div (6 + 5) =$	2) $(32 \div 4) + (12 - 5) =$
3) $(-23) + (5 \times 3) + 10 =$	4) $(-10 \times 9) \div (2^3 + 1) =$
5) $[-14(48 \div 2^4)] \div 7 =$	6) $(-5) + (63 \div 3^2) + 11 =$
7) $[15(72 \div 6^2)] - 4^2 =$	8) $4^3 + (-5 \times 2^4) + 18 =$

Find more at
bit.ly/37LBw7X

Topic	Integers and Absolute Value
Notes	✓ The absolute value of a number is its distance from zero, in either direction, on the number line. For example, the distance of 9 and -9 from zero on number line is 9. ✓ Absolute value is symbolized by vertical bars, as in $\|x\|$.
Example	**Calculate.** $\|8-3\| \times \|11-15\| =$ First calculate $\|8-3\|$, → $\|8-3\| = \|5\|$, the absolute value of 5 is 5, $\|5\| = 5$ $5 \times \|11-15\| =$ Now calculate $\|11-15\|$, → $\|11-15\| = \|-4\|$, the absolute value of -4 is 4, $\|-4\| = 4$. Then: $5 \times 4 = 20$
Your Turn!	1) $11 - \|7-12\| =$ 2) $14 - \|10-15\| - \|9\| =$
	3) $\|28\| - \dfrac{\|-35\|}{7} =$ 4) $\|-19\| + \dfrac{\|-48\|}{6} =$
	5) $\dfrac{\|4 \times -7\|}{4} \times \dfrac{\|-22\|}{2} =$ 6) $\dfrac{\|10 \times -4\|}{5} \times \|-20\| =$
	7) $\dfrac{\|-54\|}{9} \times \dfrac{\|-49\|}{7} =$ 8) $\|-38 + 9\| \times \dfrac{\|-9 \times 4\|}{6} =$

Find more at
bit.ly/3aD521u

Chapter 3: Answers

Adding and Subtracting Integers

1) −5
2) −21
3) 19
4) 18
5) −8
6) 15
7) −12
8) −9

Multiplying and Dividing Integers

1) −21
2) −7
3) 56
4) 7
5) −42
6) 5
7) −8
8) −3

Order of Operations

1) 3
2) 15
3) 2
4) −10
5) −6
6) 13
7) 14
8) 2

Integers and Absolute Values

1) 6
2) 0
3) 23
4) 27
5) 77
6) 160
7) 42
8) 174

CHAPTER
4 Ratios and Proportions

Math topics that you'll learn in this chapter:

- ✓ Simplifying Ratios
- ✓ Proportional Ratios
- ✓ Create Proportion
- ✓ Similarity and Ratios

Simplifying Ratios

Topic	Simplifying Ratios
Notes	✓ Ratios are used to make comparisons between two numbers. ✓ Ratios can be written as a fraction, using the word "to", or with a colon. ✓ You can calculate equivalent ratios by multiplying or dividing both sides of the ratio by the same number.
Examples	**Simplify.** $16:56 =$ Both numbers 16 and 56 are divisible by $8 \Rightarrow 16 \div 8 = 2, 56 \div 8 = 7$, Then: $16:56 = 2:7$ **Simplify.** $\frac{35}{45} =$ Both numbers 35 and 45 are divisible by 5, $\Rightarrow 35 \div 5 = 7, 45 \div 5 = 9$, Then: $\frac{35}{45} = \frac{7}{9}$

Your Turn!

1) $\frac{5}{45} = -$

2) $\frac{12}{36} = -$

3) $\frac{15}{60} = -$

4) $\frac{48}{56} = -$

5) $\frac{24}{96} = -$

6) $\frac{40}{72} = -$

7) $\frac{24}{80} = -$

8) $\frac{34}{136} = -$

Find more at

bit.ly/3nKwq0Z

Topic	Proportional Ratios
Notes	✓ Two ratios are proportional if they represent the same relationship. ✓ A proportion means that two ratios are equal. It can be written in two ways: $\frac{a}{b} = \frac{c}{d}$ $a:b = c:d$
Example	**Solve this proportion for** x. $\frac{4}{9} = \frac{24}{x}$ Use cross multiplication: $\frac{4}{9} = \frac{24}{x} \Rightarrow 4 \times x = 9 \times 24 \Rightarrow 4x = 216$ Divide to find x: $x = \frac{216}{4} \Rightarrow x = 54$
Your Turn!	1) $\frac{1}{5} = \frac{6}{x} \Rightarrow x =$ ____ 2) $\frac{3}{4} = \frac{15}{x} \Rightarrow x =$ ____ 3) $\frac{2}{11} = \frac{4}{x} \Rightarrow x =$ ____ 4) $\frac{4}{5} = \frac{x}{20} \Rightarrow x =$ ____ 5) $\frac{8}{9} = \frac{24}{x} \Rightarrow x =$ ____ 6) $\frac{16}{6} = \frac{x}{30} \Rightarrow x =$ ____ 7) $\frac{5}{14} = \frac{30}{x} \Rightarrow x =$ ____ 8) $\frac{4}{14} = \frac{34}{x} \Rightarrow x =$ ____

Find more at

bit.ly/37GHQxp

Topic	Create Proportion
Notes	✓ To create a proportion, simply find (or create) two equal fractions. ✓ Use cross products to solve proportions or to test whether two ratios are equal and form a proportion. $\frac{a}{b} = \frac{c}{d} \Rightarrow a \times d = c \times b$
Example	*State if this pair of ratios form a proportion.* $\frac{1}{3}$ and $\frac{12}{40}$ Use cross multiplication: $\frac{1}{3} = \frac{12}{40} \to 1 \times 40 = 12 \times 3 \to 40 = 36$, which is not correct. Therefore, this pair of ratios doesn't form a proportion.
Your Turn!	*State if each pair of ratios form a proportion.*

1) $\frac{2}{5}$ and $\frac{15}{45}$	2) $\frac{3}{4}$ and $\frac{18}{24}$
3) $\frac{2}{11}$ and $\frac{16}{88}$	4) $\frac{2}{5}$ and $\frac{54}{90}$
5) $\frac{2}{3}$ and $\frac{42}{56}$	6) $\frac{4}{5}$ and $\frac{28}{70}$
7) $\frac{2}{7}$ and $\frac{5}{40}$	8) $\frac{6}{15}$ and $\frac{18}{40}$

9) Solve.

Five pencils costs $0.60. How many pencils can you buy for $4.80? _____

Topic	Similarity and Ratios
Notes	✓ Two figures are similar if they have the same shape. ✓ Two or more figures are similar if the corresponding angles are equal, and the corresponding sides are in proportion.
Example	*Following triangles are similar. What is the value of unknown side?* **Solution:** Find the corresponding sides and write a proportion: $\frac{4}{12} = \frac{x}{9}$. Now, use cross product to solve for x: $\frac{4}{12} = \frac{x}{9} \rightarrow$ $4 \times 9 = 12 \times x \rightarrow 36 = 12x$. Divide both sides by 12. Then: $12x = 36 \rightarrow \frac{36}{12} = \frac{12x}{12} \rightarrow$ $x = 3$. The missing side is 3.
Your Turn!	1) 2) 3) 4) 5) 6)

Find more at

bit.ly/2KKKmcV

Chapter 4: Answers

Simplifying Ratios

1) $\frac{1}{9}$
2) $\frac{1}{3}$
3) $\frac{1}{4}$
4) $\frac{6}{7}$
5) $\frac{1}{4}$
6) $\frac{5}{9}$
7) $\frac{3}{10}$
8) $\frac{1}{4}$

Proportional Ratios

1) 30
2) 20
3) 22
4) 16
5) 27
6) 80
7) 84
8) 119

Create Proportion

1) No
2) Yes
3) Yes
4) No
5) No
6) No
7) No
8) No
9) 40

Similarity and Ratios

1) 24
2) 14
3) 5
4) 11
5) 10.5
6) 16

CHAPTER
5 Percentage

Math topics that you'll learn in this chapter:

- ✓ Percent Problems
- ✓ Percent of Increase and Decrease
- ✓ Discount, Tax and Tip
- ✓ Simple Interest

Percentage

Topic	Percent Problems

Notes	✓ In each percent problem, we are looking for the base, or part or the percent.
	✓ Use the following equations to find each missing section.
	   o Base = Part ÷ Percent
	   o Part = Percent × Base
	   o Percent = Part ÷ Base

Examples	**12 *is what percent of* 40?** In this problem, we are looking for the percent. Use the following equation: $Percent = Part \div Base \rightarrow Percent = 12 \div 40 = 0.3 = 30\%$ **44 *is* 20% *of what number?*** Use the following formula: $Base = Part \div Percent \rightarrow$ $Base = 44 \div 0.20 = 220$ 44 is 20% of 220.
Your Turn!	1) What is 26 percent of 450? 2) 28 is what percent of 140? 3) 40 is 5 percent of what number? 4) 32 is what percent of 800? 5) 82 is 20 percent of what number? 6) 36 is what percent of 720? 7) 66 is 22 percent of what number? 8) 48 is what percent of 800?

Find more at

bit.ly/34Gy3FL

Topic	**Percent of Increase and Decrease**
Notes	✓ Percent of change (increase or decrease) is a mathematical concept that represents the degree of change over time. ✓ To find the percentage of increase or decrease: 1- New Number – Original Number 2- The result ÷ Original Number × 100 Or use this formula: $$\text{Percent of change} = \frac{\text{new number} - \text{original number}}{\text{original number}} \times 100$$
Example	The price of a printer increases from \$20 to \$30. What is the percent increase? **Solution:** $\text{Percent of change} = \frac{\text{new number} - \text{original number}}{\text{original number}} \times 100 = \frac{30-20}{20} \times 100 = 50$ The percentage increase is 50. It means that the price of the printer increased 50%
Your Turn!	1) In a class, the number of students has been increased from 24 to 30. What is the percentage increase? _____ %
	2) The price of gasoline rose from \$4.00 to \$4.50 in one month. By what percent did the gas price rise? _____ %
	3) A shirt was originally priced at \$25.00. It went on sale for \$35.00. What was the percent that the shirt was discounted? _____ %
	4) Jason got a raise, and his hourly wage increased from \$20 to \$36. What is the percent increase? _____ %

Topic	Discount, Tax and Tip
Notes	✓ Discount = Multiply the regular price by the rate of discount ✓ Selling price = original price – discount ✓ To find tax, multiply the tax rate to the taxable amount (income, property value, etc.) ✓ To find tip, multiply the rate to the selling price.
Example	The original price of a table is $400 and the tax rate is 5%. What is the final price of the table? **Solution:** First find the tax amount. To find tax: Multiply the tax rate to the taxable amount. Tax rate is 5% or 0.05. Then: $0.05 \times 400 = 20$. The tax amount is $20. Final price is: $400 + $20 = $420

Your Turn!

1) Original price of a chair: $360 Tax: 10%, Selling price: _____	2) Original price of a computer: $700 Discount: 20%, Selling price: _____
3) Original price of a printer: $350 Tax: 10%, Selling price: _____	4) Original price of a sofa: $660 Discount: 45%, Selling price: _____
5) Original price of a mattress: $840 Tax: 15%, Selling price: _____	6) Original price of a book: $160 Discount: 40%, Selling price: _____
7) Restaurant bill: $44.00 Tip: 25%, Final amount: _____	8) Restaurant bill: $60.00 Tip: 40%, Final amount: _____

Find more at
bit.ly/2Je5lo0

Topic	Simple Interest
Notes	✓ Simple Interest: The charge for borrowing money or the return for lending it. To solve a simple interest problem, use this formula: Interest = principal x rate x time ⇒ $I = p \times r \times t$
Example	*Find simple interest for* $6,000 *investment at* 2% *for 3 years.* **Solution:** Use Interest formula: $I = prt$ ($p = \$6,000$, $r = 2\% = 0.02$ and $t = 3$) Then: $I = 6,000 \times 0.02 \times 3 = \$360$
Your Turn!	1) $250 at 4% for 3 years. Simple interest: $_____ 2) $3,400 at 6% for 2 years. Simple interest: $_____ 3) $780 at 5% for 6 years. Simple interest: $_____ 4) $3,200 at 9% for 6 years. Simple interest: $_____ 5) $1,700 at 5% for 3 years. Simple interest: $_____ 6) $520 at 6% for 5 years. Simple interest: $_____ 7) $4,300 at 4% for 6 months. Simple interest: $_____ 8) $800 at 6% for 4 months. Simple interest: $_____

Find more at
bit.ly/3nJli3D

Chapter 5: Answers

Percent Problems

1) 117
2) 20%
3) 800
4) 4%
5) 410
6) 5%
7) 300
8) 6%

Percent of Increase and Decrease

1) 25%
2) 12.5%
3) 40%
4) 80%

Discount, Tax and Tip

1) $396
2) $560
3) $385
4) $363
5) $966
6) $96
7) $55
8) $84

Simple Interest

1) $30
2) $408
3) $234
4) $1,728
5) $255
6) $156
7) $86
8) $16

CHAPTER 6: Expressions and Variables

Math topics that you'll learn in this chapter:

- ✓ Simplifying Variable Expressions
- ✓ Simplifying Polynomial Expressions
- ✓ Evaluating One Variable
- ✓ Evaluating Two Variables
- ✓ The Distributive Property

Expressions and Variables

Topic	Simplifying Variable Expressions
Notes	✓ In algebra, a variable is a letter used to stand for a number. The most common letters are: $x, y, z, a, b, c, m,$ and n. ✓ Algebraic expression is an expression contains integers, variables, and the math operations such as addition, subtraction, multiplication, division, etc. ✓ In an expression, we can combine "like" terms. (values with same variable and same power)
Example	**Simplify this expression.** $(7x + 6x + 8) = ?$ Combine like terms. Then: $(7x + 6x + 8) = 13x + 8$ **(remember you cannot combine variables and numbers).**

Your Turn!

1) $8x + 6 - 9x =$

2) $2 + 6x + 4x =$

3) $3x + 2 - 5x =$

4) $-8 - x^2 - 3x^2 =$

5) $4 + 11x^2 + 5 =$

6) $7x^2 + 5x + 3x^2 =$

7) $6x^2 - 11x^2 + 9x =$

8) $6x^2 - 7x - 2x + 3x^2 =$

9) $5x - (14 - 23x) =$

10) $11x - (54x - 40) =$

Topic	Simplifying Polynomial Expressions
Notes	✓ In mathematics, a polynomial is an expression consisting of variables and coefficients that involves only the operations of addition, subtraction, multiplication, and non–negative integer exponents of variables. $P(x) = a_n x^n + a_{n-1} x^{n-1} + \ldots + a_2 x^2 + a_1 x + z$
Example	**Simplify this expression.** $(6x^2 - x^4) - (4x^4 - 2x^2) =$ First use distributive property: → multiply $(-)$ into $(4x^4 - 2x^2)$ $(6x^2 - x^4) - (4x^4 - 2x^2) = 6x^2 - x^4 - 4x^4 + 2x^2$ Then combine "like" terms: $6x^2 - x^4 - 4x^4 + 2x^2 = 8x^2 - 5x^4$ And write in standard form: $8x^2 - 5x^4 = -5x^4 + 8x^2$

Your Turn!

1) $(x^3 + 5x^2) - (12x + 6x^2) =$	2) $(6x^5 + 3x^3) - (7x^3 + 9x^2) =$
3) $(10x^4 + 6x^2) - (5x^2 - 7x^4) =$	4) $11x - 9x^2 - 2(3x^2 + 4x^3) =$
5) $(6x^3 - 2) + 4(3x^2 - 5x^3) =$	6) $(6x^3 - 3x) - 3(2x^3 - 15x^4) =$
7) $7(2x - 3x^3) - 3(x^3 + 6x^2) =$	8) $(8x^2 - 2x) - (7x^3 + 2x^2) =$

Find more at
bit.ly/2WT5gtn

Expressions and Variables

Topic	Evaluating One Variable
Notes	✓ To evaluate one variable expression, find the variable and substitute a number for that variable. ✓ Perform the arithmetic operations.
Example	**Find the value of this expression for** $x = -5$. $-6x - 16$ **Solution:** Substitute -5 for x, then: $-6x - 16 = -6(-5) - 16 = 30 - 16 = 14$

Your Turn!		
	1) $x = 3 \Rightarrow 5x + 6 =$ ____	2) $x = -4 \Rightarrow 6x - 8 =$ ____
	3) $x = -3 \Rightarrow 7x + 2 =$ ____	4) $x = 5 \Rightarrow 6(4x + 6) =$ ____
	5) $x = 3 \Rightarrow 2(7x - 6) =$ ____	6) $x = 7 \Rightarrow 3(5x + 3) =$ ____
	7) $x = 5 \Rightarrow 8(3x + 10) =$ ____	8) $x = 6 \Rightarrow 4(2x + 9) =$ ____
	9) $x = -8 \Rightarrow -3(x + 5) =$ ____	10) $x = -4 \Rightarrow -2(4x - 6) =$ ____

Find more at
bit.ly/3ppujQZ

Topic	Evaluating Two Variables
Notes	✓ To evaluate an algebraic expression, substitute a number for each variable. ✓ Perform the arithmetic operations to find the value of the expression.
Example	**Evaluate this expression for $a = 8$ and $b = -3$. $2a - 3b$** **Solution:** Substitute 8 for a, and -3 for b, then: $2a - 3b = 2(8) - 3(-3) = 16 + 9 = 25$

Your Turn!

1) $-2a + 4b$, $a = 4$, $b = 2$ ____	2) $5x + 3y$, $x = -6$, $y = 3$ ____
3) $-3a + 4b$, $a = 3$, $b = -4$ ____	4) $6x - 3y$, $x = 2$, $y = -2$ ____
5) $3z + 11 + 4k$, $z = 5$, $k = 2$ ____	6) $6a - (8 - 4b)$, $a = 2$, $b = 3$ ____
7) $-4a + 2b$, $a = 6$, $b = 4$ ____	8) $-3a + b$, $a = -5$, $b = 8$ ____
9) $6x + 2y$, $x = -3$, $y = 7$ ____	10) $-z + 2 + 4k$, $z = -5$, $k = -4$ ____

Find more at
bit.ly/2JfrzWJ

Expressions and Variables

Topic	The Distributive Property
Notes	✓ The distributive property (or the distributive property of multiplication over addition and subtraction) simplifies and solves expressions in the form of: $a(b+c)$ or $a(b-c)$ ✓ Distributive Property rule: $$a(b+c) = ab + ac$$
Example	**Simply.** $(4)(3x - 7)$ **Solution:** Use Distributive Property rule: $a(b+c) = ab + ac$ $(4)(3x - 7) = (4 \times 3x) + (4) \times (-7) = 12x - 28$

Your Turn!

1) $(-2)(5 - 6x) =$	2) $(4 - 3x)(-4)$
3) $7(3 - 6x) =$	4) $15(2 - x) =$
5) $6(4 - 2x) =$	6) $(-3)(-4x + 2) =$
7) $(7 - 3x)(4) =$	8) $(-15x + 11)(-4) =$
9) $(-9x + 3)(-2) =$	10) $(-10x + 22)(-4) =$

Find more at
bit.ly/38qCaXs

Chapter 6: Answers

Simplifying Variable Expressions

1) $-x + 6$
2) $10x + 2$
3) $-2x + 2$
4) $-4x^2 - 8$
5) $11x^2 + 9$
6) $10x^2 + 5x$
7) $-5x^2 + 9x$
8) $9x^2 - 9x$
9) $28x - 14$
10) $-43x + 40$

Simplifying Polynomial Expressions

1) $x^3 - x^2 - 12x$
2) $6x^5 - 4x^3 - 9x^2$
3) $17x^4 + x^2$
4) $-8x^3 - 15x^2 + 11x$
5) $-14x^3 + 12x^2 - 2$
6) $45x^4 - 3x$
7) $-24x^3 - 18x^2 + 14x$
8) $-7x^3 - 6x^2 - 2x$

Evaluating One Variable

1) 21
2) -32
3) -19
4) 156
5) 30
6) 114
7) 200
8) 84
9) 9
10) 44

Evaluating Two Variables

1) 0
2) -21
3) -25
4) 18
5) 34
6) 16
7) -16
8) 23
9) -4
10) -9

The Distributive Property

1) $12x - 10$
2) $12x - 16$
3) $-42x + 21$
4) $-15x + 30$
5) $-12x + 24$
6) $12x - 6$
7) $-12x + 28$
8) $60x - 44$
9) $18x - 6$
10) $40x - 88$

CHAPTER 7: Equations and Inequalities

Math topics that you'll learn in this chapter:

- ✓ One-Step Equations
- ✓ Multi-Step Equations
- ✓ System of Equations
- ✓ Graphing Single–Variable Inequalities
- ✓ One-Step Inequalities
- ✓ Multi-Step Inequalities

Equations and Inequalities

Topic	One–Step Equations
Notes	✓ You only need to perform one Math operation in order to solve the one-step equations. ✓ To solve one-step equation, find the inverse (opposite) operation is being performed. ✓ The inverse operations are: - Addition and subtraction - Multiplication and division
Example	**Solve this equation.** $x + 48 = 63 \Rightarrow x = ?$ Here, the operation is addition and its inverse operation is subtraction. To solve this equation, subtract 48 from both sides of the equation: $x + 48 - 48 = 63 - 48$ Then simplify: $x + 48 - 48 = 63 - 48 \Rightarrow x = 15$
Your Turn!	1) $x - 14 = 54 \Rightarrow x =$ ____ 2) $18 = 12 + x \Rightarrow x =$ ____
	3) $x - 24 = 58 \Rightarrow x =$ ____ 4) $x + 16 = 29 \Rightarrow x =$ ____
	5) $6x = 30 \Rightarrow x =$ ____ 6) $\frac{x}{5} = -9 \Rightarrow x =$ ____
	7) $12x = 96 \Rightarrow x =$ ____ 8) $\frac{x}{16} = -3 \Rightarrow x =$ ____

Find more at
bit.ly/37Jq0tK

Topic	Multi –Step Equations
Notes	✓ Combine "like" terms on one side. ✓ Bring variables to one side by adding or subtracting. ✓ Simplify using the inverse of addition or subtraction. ✓ Simplify further by using the inverse of multiplication or division. ✓ Check your solution by plugging the value of the variable into the original equation.
Example	**Solve this equation for x.** $3x - 4 = 17$ **Solution:** The inverse of subtraction is addition. Add 4 to both sides of the equation. Then: $3x - 4 = 17 \Rightarrow 3x - 4 = 17 + 4$ $\Rightarrow 3x = 21$. Now, divide both sides by 3, then: $\frac{3x}{3} = \frac{21}{3} \Rightarrow x = 7$ Now, check the solution: $x = 7 \Rightarrow 3x - 4 = 17 \Rightarrow 3(7) - 4 = 17 \Rightarrow 21 - 4 = 17$ The answer $x = 7$ is correct.
Your Turn!	

1) $6x - 18 = 12 \Rightarrow x =$	2) $16 - 4x = -5 + 3x \Rightarrow x =$
3) $2(2 - 3x) = 28 \Rightarrow x =$	4) $14 + 2x = -6 - 8x \Rightarrow x =$
5) $-4(6 + x) = 8 \Rightarrow x =$	6) $14 - 3x = -2 - 7x \Rightarrow x =$
7) $16 = -(x - 7) \Rightarrow x =$	8) $14 - 6x = -4 - 3x \Rightarrow x =$

Find more at

bit.ly/3nQbSEB

Topic	System of Equations
Notes	✓ A system of equations contains two equations and two variables. For example, consider the system of equations: $x - 2y = -2, x + 2y = 10$ ✓ The easiest way to solve a system of equation is using the elimination method. The elimination method uses the addition property of equality. You can add the same value to each side of an equation. ✓ For the first equation above, you can add $x + 2y$ to the left side and 10 to the right side of the first equation: $x - 2y + (x + 2y) = -2 + 10$. Now, if you simplify, you get: $x - 2y + (x + 2y) = -2 + 10 \to 2x = 8 \to x = 4$. Now, substitute 4 for the x in the first equation: $4 - 2y = -2$. By solving this equation, $y = 3$
Example	What is the value of x and y in this system of equations? $\begin{cases} 4x - y = 18 \\ -x + 4y = 3 \end{cases}$ **Solution:** Solving System of Equations by Elimination: $\begin{array}{r} 4x - y = 18 \\ \underline{-x + 4y = 3} \end{array}$ Multiply the second equation by 4, then add it to the first equation. $\begin{array}{r} 4x - y = 18 \\ \underline{4(-x + 4y = 3)} \end{array} \Rightarrow \begin{array}{r} 4x - y = 18 \\ \underline{-4x + 16y = 12} \end{array} \Rightarrow 15y = 30 \Rightarrow y = 2$. Now, substitute 2 for y in the first equation and solve for x. $4x - (2) = 18 \Rightarrow 4x = 20 \Rightarrow x = 5$
Your Turn!	1) $3x - y = 7$ $2x + y = 13$ $x = $ ___ $y = $ ___ 2) $4x + 8y = -24$ $-4x - 2y = -12$ $x = $ ___ $y = $ ___
	3) $x + y = -5$ $3x + 2y = 12$ $x = $ ___ $y = $ ___ 4) $y = x - 1$ $y = 2x - 3$ $x = $ ___ $y = $ ___
	5) $7x + y = 50$ $14x - 2y = -44$ $x = $ ___ $y = $ ___ 6) $4x + 2y = 14$ $7x - 3y = -8$ $x = $ ___ $y = $ ___

Topic	Graphing Single–Variable Inequalities
Notes	✓ An inequality compares two expressions using an inequality sign. ✓ Inequality signs are: "less than" <, "greater than" >, "less than or equal to" ≤, and "greater than or equal to" ≥. ✓ To graph a single–variable inequality, find the value of the inequality on the number line. ✓ For less than (<) or greater than (>) draw open circle on the value of the variable. If there is an equal sign too, then use filled circle. ✓ Draw an arrow to the right for greater or to the left for less than.
Example	**Draw a graph for this inequality.** $x < 4$ **Solution:** Since, the variable is less than 4, then we need to find 4 in the number line and draw an open circle on it. Then, draw an arrow to the left.

Your Turn!

1) $x < 1$

2) $x \geq -5$

3) $x \geq -4$

4) $x \leq 6$

5) $x > -6$

6) $5 > x$

7) $-2 \leq x$

8) $x > 3$

Find more at
bit.ly/3aJ4GGo

Topic	One–Step Inequalities
Notes	✓ Inequality signs are: "less than" <, "greater than" >, "less than or equal to" ≤, and "greater than or equal to" ≥. ✓ You only need to perform one Math operation in order to solve the one-step inequalities. ✓ To solve one-step inequalities, find the inverse (opposite) operation is being performed. ✓ For dividing or multiplying both sides by negative numbers, flip the direction of the inequality sign.
Example	**Solve this inequality.** $x + 18 < 56 \Rightarrow$ _____ Here, the operation is addition and its inverse operation is subtraction. To solve this inequality, subtract 18 from both sides of the inequality: $x + 18 - 18 < 56 - 18$ Then simplify: $x < 38$

Your Turn!

1) $4x < -8 \Rightarrow$ _____	2) $x - 9 > 32 \Rightarrow$ _____
3) $-4x \geq 48 \Rightarrow$ _____	4) $x - 12 \leq 8 \Rightarrow$ _____
5) $\frac{x}{5} \geq -7 \Rightarrow$ _____	6) $54 < 6x \Rightarrow$ _____
7) $84 \leq 12x \Rightarrow$ _____	8) $\frac{x}{9} > -9 \Rightarrow$ _____

Find more at

bit.ly/3rrElgL

Topic	Multi – Step Inequalities
Notes	✓ Isolate the variable. ✓ Simplify using the inverse of addition or subtraction. ✓ Simplify further by using the inverse of multiplication or division. ✓ For dividing or multiplying both sides by negative numbers, flip the direction of the inequality sign.
Example	**Solve this inequality.** $4x + 10 \leq 26$ **Solution:** First subtract 10 from both sides: $4x + 10 - 10 \leq 26 - 10$ Then simplify: $4x + 10 - 10 \leq 26 - 10 \rightarrow 4x \leq 16$ Now divide both sides by 4: $\frac{4x}{4} \leq \frac{16}{4} \rightarrow x \leq 4$

Your Turn!

1) $2x + 6 < 30 \rightarrow$ _____

2) $4x - 8 \leq 12 \rightarrow$ _____

3) $6x - 2 \leq 22 \rightarrow$ _____

4) $18 - 5x \geq -7 \rightarrow$ _____

5) $22 - 4x \geq -10 \rightarrow$ _____

6) $6x - 10 \leq 20 \rightarrow$ _____

7) $8 + 9x < 62 \rightarrow$ _____

8) $8 - 9x < 89 \rightarrow$ _____

Find more at

bit.ly/2WK1xOr

Chapter 7: Answers

One-Step Equations

1) 68
2) 6
3) 82
4) 13
5) 5
6) −45
7) 8
8) −48

Multi-Step Equations

1) 5
2) 3
3) −4
4) −2
5) −8
6) −4
7) −9
8) 6

System of Equations

1) $x = 4, y = 5$
2) $x = 6, y = -6$
3) $x = 22, y = -27$
4) $x = 2, y = 1$
5) $x = 2, y = 36$
6) $x = 1, y = 5$

Graphing Single-Variable Inequalities

1)

2)
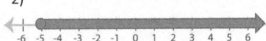

3)
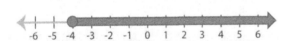

4)

5)

6)
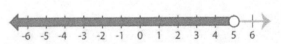

7)

8)

One-Step Inequalities

1) $x < -2$
2) $x > 41$
3) $x \leq -12$
4) $x \leq 20$
5) $x \geq -35$
6) $9 < x$
7) $7 \leq x$
8) $x > -81$

Multi-Step Inequalities

1) $x < 12$
2) $x \leq 5$
3) $x \leq 4$
4) $x \leq 5$
5) $x \leq 8$
6) $x \leq 5$
7) $x < 6$
8) $x > -9$

CHAPTER
8 Lines and Slope

Math topics that you'll learn in this chapter:

- ✓ Finding Slope
- ✓ Graphing Lines Using Slope–Intercept Form
- ✓ Writing Linear Equations
- ✓ Finding Midpoint
- ✓ Finding Distance of Two Points

Lines and Slope

Topic	Finding Slope
Notes	- The slope of a line represents the direction of a line on the coordinate plane. - A line on coordinate plane can be drawn by connecting two points. - To find the slope of a line, we need two points. - The slope of a line with two points A (x_1, y_1) and B (x_2, y_2) can be found by using this formula: $\frac{y_2 - y_1}{x_2 - x_1} = \frac{rise}{run}$ - The equation of a line is typically written as $y = mx + b$ where m is the slope and b is the y-intercept.
Examples	**Find the slope of the line through these two points:** $(5, -10)$ **and** $(9, 6)$. **Solution:** Slope = $\frac{y_2 - y_1}{x_2 - x_1}$. Let (x_1, y_1) be $(5, -10)$ and (x_2, y_2) be $(9, 6)$. Then: slope = $\frac{y_2 - y_1}{x_2 - x_1} = \frac{6 - (-10)}{9 - 5} = \frac{6 + 10}{4} = \frac{16}{4} = 4$ **Find the slope of the line with equation** $y = 3x - 7$ **Solution:** when the equation of a line is written in the form of $y = mx + b$, the slope is m. In this line: $y = 3x - 7$, the slope is 3.

Your Turn!

1) $(1, 2), (6, 7)$

   Slope = ___

2) $(-4, 2), (0, 6)$

   Slope = ___

3) $(-3, -1), (-4, 2)$

   Slope = ___

4) $(-5, 3), (5, -1)$

   Slope = ___

5) $y = 2x + 11$

   Slope = ___

6) $y = -5x + 9$

   Slope = ___

Find more at

bit.ly/3nMJYJv

Topic	Graphing Lines Using Slope–Intercept Form
Notes	✓ Slope–intercept form of a line: given the slope m and the y–intercept (the intersection of the line and y–axis) b, then the equation of the line is: $$y = mx + b$$
Example	**Sketch the graph of** $y = -3x - 2$. **Solution:** To graph this line, we need to find two points. When x is zero the value of y is -2. And when y is zero the value of x is $-\frac{2}{3}$. $x = 0 \to y = -3(0) - 2 = -2, y = 0 \to 0 = -3x - 2 \to x = -\frac{2}{3}$ Now, we have two points: $(0, -3)$ and $(-\frac{2}{3}, 0)$. Find the points and graph the line. Remember that the slope of the line is $-\frac{2}{3}$.
Your Turn!	1) $y = -2x + 1$ 2) $y = -x - 6$

Topic	Writing Linear Equations
Notes	✓ The equation of a line: $y = mx + b$ ✓ Identify the slope. ✓ Find the y–intercept. This can be done by substituting the slope and the coordinates of a point (x, y) on the line.
Example	**Write the equation of the line through $(2, 1)$ and $(-1, 7)$.** **Solution:** Slope $= \frac{y_2-y_1}{x_2-x_1} = \frac{7-1}{-1-2} = \frac{6}{-3} = -2 \to m = -2$ To find the value of b, you can use either points. The answer will be the same: $y = -2x + b$ $(2, 1) \to 1 = -2(2) + b \to b = 5$ $(-1, 7) \to 7 = -2(-1) + b \to b = 5$ The equation of the line is: $y = -2x + 5$

Your Turn!

1) through: $(-1, 2), (1, 8)$

   $y =$

2) through: $(7, 1), (5, 9)$

   $y =$

3) through: $(3, -3), (8, 2)$

   $y =$

4) through: $(-2, 2), (4, -10)$

   $y =$

5) through: $(4, -6), (-5, 12)$

   $y =$

6) through: $(3, -3), (-2, 7)$

   $y =$

7) through $(-2, 4)$, Slope: 3

   $y =$

8) through $(5, -2)$, Slope: -6

   $y =$

Topic	Finding Midpoint
Notes	✓ The middle of a line segment is its midpoint. ✓ The Midpoint of two endpoints A (x_1, y_1) and B (x_2, y_2) can be found using this formula: $M\left(\frac{x_1+x_2}{2}, \frac{y_1+y_2}{2}\right)$
Example	Find the midpoint of the line segment with the given endpoints. $(2, -2), (4, 8)$ **Solution:** Midpoint $= \left(\frac{x_1+x_2}{2}, \frac{y_1+y_2}{2}\right) \rightarrow (x_1, y_1) = (2, -2)$ and $(x_2, y_2) = (4, 8)$ Midpoint $= \left(\frac{2+4}{2}, \frac{-2+8}{2}\right) \rightarrow \left(\frac{6}{2}, \frac{6}{2}\right) \rightarrow M(3, 3)$
Your Turn!	1) $(3, 2), (-7, 2)$ **Midpoint** = (__, __)	2) $(4, 1), (10, 5)$ **Midpoint** = (__, __)
	3) $(-3, 3), (5, 3)$ **Midpoint** = (__, __)	4) $(8, 3), (-4, 5)$ **Midpoint** = (__, __)
	5) $(5, 4), (-1, 2)$ **Midpoint** = (__, __)	6) $(6, -4), (6, 6)$ **Midpoint** = (__, __)
	7) $(9, 4), (-1, -6)$ **Midpoint** = (__, __)	8) $(7, 4), (-1, 10)$ **Midpoint** = (__, __)
	9) $(-2, 7), (4, -5)$ **Midpoint** = (__, __)	10) $(-16, -3), (2, -5)$ **Midpoint** = (__, __)

Find more at
bit.ly/3nPdnTq

Lines and Slope

Topic	Finding Distance of Two Points
Notes	✓ Use this formula to find the distance of two points A (x_1, y_1) and B (x_2, y_2): $$d = \sqrt{(x_2 - x_1)^2 + (y_2 - y_1)^2}$$
Example	**Find the distance of two points** $(8, 2)$ and $(-6, 2)$. **Solution:** *Use distance of two points formula:* $d = \sqrt{(x_2 - x_1)^2 + (y_2 - y_1)^2}$ $(x_1, y_1) = (8, 2)$, and $(x_2, y_2) = (-6, 2)$ Then: $d = \sqrt{(x_2 - x_1)^2 + (y_2 - y_1)^2} \rightarrow d = \sqrt{(-6 - (8))^2 + (2 - 2)^2} = \sqrt{(14)^2 + (0)^2} = \sqrt{196 + 0} = \sqrt{196} = 14$
Your Turn!	1) $(0, 0), (6, 8)$ Distance = ____ 2) $(-6, 12), (-6, 10)$ Distance = ____
	3) $(9, 4), (-5, 4)$ Distance = ____ 4) $(8, 9), (3, -3)$ Distance = ____
	5) $(-5, 24), (-5, 20)$ Distance = ____ 6) $(-2, 5), (4, -3)$ Distance = ____
	7) $(4, 4), (7, 8)$ Distance = ____ 8) $(4, -1), (14, 23)$ Distance = ____

Chapter 8: Answers

Finding Slope

1) 1
2) 1
3) −3
4) $-\dfrac{2}{5}$
5) 2
6) −5

Graphing Lines Using Slope-Intercept Form

1)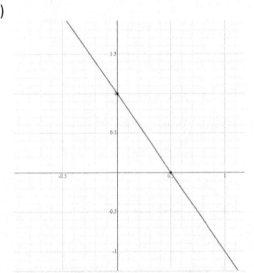

2)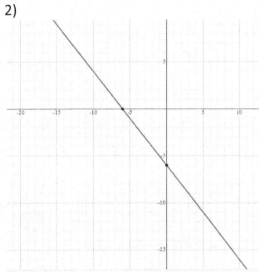

Writing Linear Equations

1) $y = 3x + 5$
2) $y = -4x + 29$
3) $y = x - 6$
4) $y = -2x - 2$
5) $y = -2x + 2$
6) $y = -2x + 3$
7) $y = 3x + 10$
8) $y = -6x + 28$

Finding Midpoint

1) $(-2, 2)$
2) $(7, 3)$
3) $(1, 3)$
4) $(2, 4)$
5) $(2, 3)$
6) $(6, 1)$
7) $(4, -1)$
8) $(3, 7)$
9) $(1, 1)$
10) $(-7, -4)$

Finding Distance of Two points

1) 10
2) 2
3) 14
4) 13
5) 4
6) 10
7) 5
8) 26

CHAPTER 9
Exponents and Variables

Math topics that you'll learn in this chapter:

- ✓ Multiplication Property of Exponents
- ✓ Division Property of Exponents
- ✓ Powers of Products and Quotients
- ✓ Zero and Negative Exponents
- ✓ Negative Exponents and Negative Bases
- ✓ Scientific Notation
- ✓ Radicals

Exponents and Variables

Topic	Multiplication Property of Exponents
Notes	✓ Exponents are shorthand for repeated multiplication of the same number by itself. For example, instead of 2×2, we can write 2^2. For $3 \times 3 \times 3 \times 3$, we can write 3^4 ✓ In algebra, a variable is a letter used to stand for a number. The most common letters are: $x, y, z, a, b, c, m,$ and n. ✓ Exponent's rules: $x^a \times x^b = x^{a+b}$, $\frac{x^a}{x^b} = x^{a-b}$ $(x^a)^b = x^{a \times b}$ $(xy)^a = x^a \times y^a$ $\left(\frac{a}{b}\right)^c = \frac{a^c}{b^c}$
Example	**Multiply.** $6x^5 \times 4x^2$ Use Exponent's rules: $x^a \times x^b = x^{a+b} \rightarrow x^5 \times x^2 = x^{5+2} = x^7$ Then: $6x^5 \times 4x^2 = 24x^7$

Your Turn!

1) $x^3 \times 4x =$	2) $5x^4 \times x^3 =$
3) $5x^3 \times 2x^4 =$	4) $7x^2 \times 9xy =$
5) $4x^7y \times 3x^2y^4 =$	6) $5x^3y^2 \times 6x^2y^6 =$
7) $9x^2y \times 3x^5y^6 =$	8) $8x^6 \times 4x^8y^4 =$
9) $8x^3y^7 \times 5x^5y^2 =$	10) $2x^7y^3 \times 9xy^2 =$

Find more at
bit.ly/34AWHr1

Topic	Division Property of Exponents
Notes	✓ For division of exponents use these formulas: $\frac{x^a}{x^b} = x^{a-b}$, $x \neq 0$ $\frac{x^a}{x^b} = \frac{1}{x^{b-a}}$, $x \neq 0$, $\quad \frac{1}{x^b} = x^{-b}$
Example	**Simplify.** $\frac{4x^4 y}{36x^2 y^2}$ First cancel the common factor: $4 \to \frac{4x^4 y}{36x^2 y^2} = \frac{x^4 y}{9x^2 y^2}$ Use Exponent's rules: $\frac{x^a}{x^b} = x^{a-b} \to \frac{x^4}{x^2} = x^{4-2} = x^2$ Then: $\frac{4x^4 y}{36x^2 y^2} = \frac{xy}{9y^2} \to$ now cancel the common factor: $y \to \frac{xy}{9y^2} = \frac{x}{9y}$
Your Turn!	1) $\frac{3^6}{3^2} =$ 2) $\frac{5x}{15x^4} =$ 3) $\frac{6x^2}{2x^5} =$ 4) $\frac{14x^3}{21x^7} =$ 5) $\frac{12x^4}{18y^5} =$ 6) $\frac{28xy^4}{7x^5 y^3} =$ 7) $\frac{2x^3 y^8}{5xy^2} =$ 8) $\frac{4x^3 y^7}{10x^4} =$ 9) $\frac{6x^3}{24x^7 y^5} =$ 10) $\frac{16y^6 x^4}{32y^2 x^9} =$

Find more at

bit.ly/37JAclZ

Exponents and Variables

Topic	Powers of Products and Quotients
Notes	✓ For any nonzero numbers a and b and any integer x, $$(ab)^x = a^x \times b^x, \left(\frac{a}{b}\right)^c = \frac{a^c}{b^c}$$
Example	**Simplify.** $\left(\frac{3x^4}{x}\right)^2$ First cancel the common factor: $x \rightarrow \left(\frac{3x^4}{x}\right)^2 = (3x^3)^2$ Use Exponent's rules: $(ab)^x = a^x \times b^x$ Then: $(3x^3)^2 = (3)^2(x^3)^2 = 9x^6$

Your Turn!

1) $(2x^3 x^2)^3 =$	2) $(3x^4 \times 4x)^2 =$
3) $(9x^{10} y^3)^2 =$	4) $(8x^7 y^3)^2 =$
5) $(6x^5 y^6)^3 =$	6) $(2x \times 4y^6)^2 =$
7) $\left(\frac{9x}{x^3}\right)^2 =$	8) $\left(\frac{x^5 y^6}{x^2 y^2}\right)^3 =$
9) $\left(\frac{28x}{4x^7}\right)^2 =$	10) $\left(\frac{32x^6}{40x^4 y^3}\right)^2 =$

Topic	Zero and Negative Exponents
Notes	✓ A negative exponent is the reciprocal of that number with a positive exponent. $(3)^{-2} = \frac{1}{3^2}$ ✓ Zero-Exponent Rule: $a^0 = 1$, this means that anything raised to the zero power is 1. For example: $(28x^2y)^0 = 1$
Example	**Evaluate.** $\left(\frac{1}{4}\right)^{-2} =$ Use negative exponent's rule: $\left(\frac{1}{x^a}\right)^{-2} = (x^a)^2 \rightarrow \left(\frac{1}{4}\right)^{-2} = (4)^2 =$ Then: $(4)^2 = 16$

Your Turn!

1) $2^{-5} =$	2) $3^{-3} =$
3) $5^{-3} =$	4) $1^{-7} =$
5) $6^{-3} =$	6) $4^{-3} =$
7) $10^{-4} =$	8) $7^{-3} =$
9) $\left(\frac{1}{9}\right)^{-1} =$	10) $\left(\frac{1}{7}\right)^{-4} =$

Find more at

bit.ly/3rnkh4v

Topic	Negative Exponents and Negative Bases
Notes	✓ Make the power positive. A negative exponent is the reciprocal of that number with a positive exponent. ✓ The parenthesis is important! 5^{-2} is not the same as $(-5)^{-2}$ $$(-5)^{-2} = -\frac{1}{5^2} \text{ and } (-5)^{-2} = +\frac{1}{5^2}$$
Example	**Simplify.** $\left(-\frac{5x}{6yz}\right)^{-3} =$ Use negative exponent's rule: $\left(\frac{x^a}{x^b}\right)^{-2} = \left(\frac{x^b}{x^a}\right)^{2} \rightarrow \left(-\frac{5x}{6yz}\right)^{-3} = \left(-\frac{6yz}{5x}\right)^{3}$ Now use exponent's rule: $\left(\frac{a}{b}\right)^c = \frac{a^c}{b^c} \rightarrow \left(-\frac{6yz}{5x}\right)^3 = -\frac{6^3 y^3 z^3}{5^3 x^3} = -\frac{216 y^3 z^3}{125 x^3}$

Your Turn!

1) $-3x^{-4}y^{-2} =$	2) $20x^{-7}y^{-2} =$
3) $18a^{-9}b^{-8} =$	4) $-10x^3 y^{-4} =$
5) $-\dfrac{27}{x^{-6}} =$	6) $\dfrac{8b}{-9c^{-5}} =$
7) $\dfrac{10ab}{a^{-4}b^{-2}} =$	8) $-\dfrac{6n^{-2}}{18p^{-4}} =$
9) $\dfrac{48ab^{-1}}{-3c^{-4}} =$	10) $\left(\dfrac{9a}{6c}\right)^{-3} =$

Topic	Scientific Notation
Notes	✓ It is used to write very big or very small numbers in decimal form. ✓ In scientific notation all numbers are written in the form of: $$m \times 10^n$$ | Decimal notation	Scientific notation | |---|---| | 3 | 3×10^0 | | $-45,000$ | -4.5×10^4 | | 0.3 | 3×10^{-1} | | 2,122.456 | 2.122456×10^3 |
Example	**Write 0.00049 in scientific notation.** First, move the decimal point to the right so that you have a number that is between 1 and 10. Then: $m = 4.9$ Now, determine how many places the decimal moved in step 1 by the power of 10. Then: 10^{-4} → When the decimal moved to the right, the exponent is negative. Then: $0.00049 = 4.9 \times 10^{-4}$
Your Turn!	1) $0.000281 =$ 2) $0.00056 =$ 3) $37,000,000 =$ 4) $19,000 =$ 5) $4 \times 10^{-1} =$ 6) $8 \times 10^{-2} =$ 7) $2.6 \times 10^4 =$ 8) $7.2 \times 10^{-5} =$

Exponents and Variables

Topic	Radicals
Notes	✓ If n is a positive integer and x is a real number, then: $\sqrt[n]{x} = x^{\frac{1}{n}}$, $\sqrt[n]{xy} = x^{\frac{1}{n}} \times y^{\frac{1}{n}}$, $\sqrt[n]{\frac{x}{y}} = \frac{x^{\frac{1}{n}}}{y^{\frac{1}{n}}}$, and $\sqrt[n]{x} \times \sqrt[n]{y} = \sqrt[n]{xy}$ ✓ A square root of x is a number r whose square is: $r^2 = x$ (r is a square root of x. ✓ To add and subtract radicals, we need to have the same values under the radical. For example: $\sqrt{3} + \sqrt{3} = 2\sqrt{3}$, $3\sqrt{5} - \sqrt{5} = 2\sqrt{5}$
Example	**Evaluate.** $\sqrt{18} + \sqrt{8} =$ **Solution:** Since we do not have the same values under the radical, we cannot add these two radicals. But we can simplify each radical. $\sqrt{18} = \sqrt{9} \times \sqrt{2} = 3\sqrt{2}$ and $\sqrt{8} = \sqrt{4} \times \sqrt{2} = 2\sqrt{2}$ Now, we have the same values under the radical. Then: $\sqrt{18} + \sqrt{8} = 3\sqrt{2} + 2\sqrt{2} = 5\sqrt{2}$
Your Turn!	1) $\sqrt{5} \times \sqrt{5} =$ 2) $\sqrt{8} \times \sqrt{2} =$
	3) $\sqrt{3} \times \sqrt{12} =$ 4) $\sqrt{48} \div \sqrt{3} =$
	5) $\sqrt{2} + \sqrt{18} =$ 6) $\sqrt{28} - \sqrt{7} =$
	7) $4\sqrt{5} - 2\sqrt{5} =$ 8) $7\sqrt{7} \times 3\sqrt{7} =$

Find more at
bit.ly/2WEATqr

Chapter 9: Answers

Multiplication Property of Exponents

1) $4x^4$
2) $5x^7$
3) $10x^7$
4) $63x^3y$
5) $12x^9y^5$
6) $30x^5y^8$
7) $27x^7y^7$
8) $32x^{14}y^4$
9) $40x^8y^9$
10) $18x^8y^5$

Division Property of Exponents

1) 3^4
2) $\dfrac{1}{3x^3}$
3) $\dfrac{3}{x^3}$
4) $\dfrac{2}{3x^4}$
5) $\dfrac{2x^4}{3y^5}$
6) $\dfrac{4y}{x^4}$
7) $\dfrac{2x^2y^6}{5}$
8) $\dfrac{2y^7}{5x}$
9) $\dfrac{1}{4x^4y^5}$
10) $\dfrac{y^4}{2x^5}$

Powers of Products and Quotients

1) $8x^{15}$
2) $144x^{10}$
3) $81x^{20}y^6$
4) $64x^{14}y^6$
5) $216x^{15}y^{18}$
6) $64x^2y^{12}$
7) $\dfrac{81}{x^4}$
8) x^9y^{12}
9) $\dfrac{49}{x^{12}}$
10) $\dfrac{16x^4}{25y^6}$

Zero and Negative Exponents

1) $\dfrac{1}{32}$
2) $\dfrac{1}{27}$
3) $\dfrac{1}{125}$
4) 1
5) $\dfrac{1}{216}$
6) $\dfrac{1}{64}$
7) $\dfrac{1}{10,000}$
8) $\dfrac{1}{343}$
9) 9
10) $2,401$

Exponents and Variables

Negative Exponents and Negative Bases

1) $-\dfrac{3}{x^4 y^2}$

2) $\dfrac{20}{x^7 y^2}$

3) $\dfrac{18}{a^9 b^8}$

4) $-\dfrac{10x^3}{y^4}$

5) $-27x^6$

6) $-\dfrac{8bc^5}{9}$

7) $10a^5 b^3$

8) $-\dfrac{p^4}{3n^2}$

9) $-\dfrac{16ac^4}{b}$

10) $\dfrac{8c^3}{27a^3}$

Scientific Notation

1) 2.81×10^{-4}

2) 5.6×10^{-4}

3) 3.7×10^7

4) 1.9×10^4

5) 0.4

6) 0.08

7) $26{,}000$

8) 0.000072

Radicals

1) 5

2) 4

3) 6

4) 4

5) $4\sqrt{2}$

6) $\sqrt{7}$

7) $2\sqrt{5}$

8) 147

Chapter 10 Polynomials

Math topics that you'll learn in this chapter:

- ✓ Simplifying Polynomials
- ✓ Adding and Subtracting Polynomials
- ✓ Multiplying Binomials
- ✓ Multiplying and Dividing Monomials
- ✓ Multiplying a Polynomial and a Monomial
- ✓ Multiplying Monomials
- ✓ Factoring Trinomials

Topic	Simplifying Polynomials
Notes	✓ Find "like" terms. (they have same variables with same power). ✓ Use "FOIL". (First–Out–In–Last) for binomials: $(x + a)(x + b) = x^2 + (b + a)x + ab$ ✓ Add or Subtract "like" terms using order of operation.
Example	**Simplify this expression.** $(x + 2)(x - 5) =$ **Solution:** First apply FOIL method: $(a + b)(c + d) = ac + ad + bc + bd$ $(x + 2)(x - 5) = x^2 - 5x + 2x - 10$ Now combine like terms: $x^2 - 5x + 2x - 10 = x^2 - 3x - 10$

Your Turn!

1) $-(5x - 2) =$

2) $2(4x + 9) =$

3) $4x(2x - 5) =$

4) $6x(2x + 7) =$

5) $-3x(4x + 2) + 6x =$

6) $-5x(9x - 2) - 2x^2 =$

7) $(x + 1)(x + 5) =$

8) $(x + 6)(x + 8) =$

9) $-3x^2 + 8x^3 + 12x^2 =$

10) $-7x^5 + 9x^4 + 4x^5 =$

Topic	Adding and Subtracting Polynomials
Notes	✓ Adding polynomials is just a matter of combining like terms, with some order of operations considerations thrown in. ✓ Be careful with the minus signs, and don't confuse addition and multiplication!
Example	**Simplify the expressions.** $(5x^2 - 2x^3) - (4x^3 - 8x^2) =$ **Solution:** First use Distributive Property: $-(4x^3 - 8x^2) = -4x^3 + 8x^2$ $\rightarrow (5x^2 - 2x^3) - (4x^3 - 8x^2) = 5x^2 - 2x^3 - 4x^3 + 8x^2$ Now combine like terms: $5x^2 - 2x^3 - 4x^3 + 8x^2 = -6x^3 + 13x^2$

Your Turn!

1) $(x^2 - 2x) + (2x^2 - 5) =$ _____

2) $(9x^3 + 3x) - (x^3 + 3) =$ _____

3) $(x^2 - 7x) + (2x^2 - 4) =$ _____

4) $(9x^2 - 3) - (4x^2 + 2) =$ _____

5) $(5x^2 + 3) - (4 - 3x^2) =$ _____

6) $(x^3 + x^2) - (x^3 - 8) =$ _____

7) $(7x^3 - 3x) - (x - x^3) =$ _____

8) $(x - 3x^4) - (2x^4 + 7x) =$ _____

Find more at
bit.ly/2KUqHqQ

9) $(6x^3 + 3) - (4 - 2x^3) =$ _____

10) $(7x^2 + 3x^3) - (9x^3 + 4) =$

Topic	Multiplying Binomials
Notes	✓ A binomial is a polynomial that is the sum or the difference of two terms, each of which is a monomial. ✓ To multiply two binomials, use "FOIL" method. (First–Out–In–Last) $(x + a)(x + b) = x \times x + x \times b + a \times x + a \times b = x^2 + bx + ax + ab$
Example	**Multiply.** $(x - 3)(x + 7) =$ **Solution:** Use "FOIL". (First–Out–In–Last): $(x - 3)(x + 7) =$ $x^2 + 7x - 3x - 21$ Then simplify: $x^2 + 7x - 3x - 21 = x^2 + 4x - 21$
Your Turn!	1) $(x + 3)(x + 3) =$ _____	2) $(x + 5)(x + 3) =$ _____
	3) $(x - 2)(x + 6) =$ _____	4) $(x - 5)(x - 7) =$ _____
	5) $(x + 9)(x + 4) =$ _____	6) $(x + 6)(x + 8) =$ _____
	7) $(x - 7)(x - 5) =$ _____	8) $(x - 6)(x - 6) =$ _____
	9) $(x + 9)(x - 4) =$ _____	10) $(x - 8)(x + 3) =$ _____

Topic	**Multiplying and Dividing Monomials**
Notes	✓ When you divide or multiply two monomials you need to divide or multiply their coefficients and then divide or multiply their variables. ✓ In case of exponents with the same base, you need to subtract their powers. ✓ Exponent's rules: $$x^a \times x^b = x^{a+b}, \quad \frac{x^a}{x^b} = x^{a-b}$$ $$\frac{1}{x^b} = x^{-b}, \quad (x^a)^b = x^{a \times b}$$ $$(xy)^a = x^a \times y^a$$
Example	**Divide expressions.** $\frac{-16x^4y^5}{2xy^2} =$ **Solution:** Use exponents' division rule: $\frac{x^a}{x^b} = x^{a-b}, \frac{x^4}{x} = x^{4-1} = x^3$ and $\frac{y^5}{y^2} = y^3$ Then: $\frac{-16x^4y^5}{2xy^2} = -8x^3y^3$
Your Turn!	1) $(x^5y)(xy^2) =$ _____ 2) $(x^6y^2)(x^2y^5) =$ _____
	3) $(x^6y^4)(2x^5y^3) =$ _____ 4) $(4x^3y^4)(4x^6y^6) =$ _____
	5) $(-7x^5y^7)(6x^6y^8) =$ _____ 6) $(-6x^8y^3)(9x^7y^4) =$ _____
Find more at bit.ly/2WHp4Q4	7) $\frac{48x^7y^6}{8x^5y^2} =$ _____ 8) $\frac{-54x^{12}y^{15}}{9x^8y^6} =$ _____

Topic	Multiplying a Polynomial and a Monomial
Notes	✓ When multiplying monomials, use the product rule for exponents. $x^a \times x^b = x^{a+b}$ ✓ When multiplying a monomial by a polynomial, use the distributive property. $$a \times (b + c) = a \times b + a \times c = ab + ac$$ $$a \times (b - c) = a \times b - a \times c = ab - ac$$
Example	**Multiply expressions.** $3x(4x - 3) =$ **Solution:** Use Distributive Property: $3x(4x - 3) = 3x \times 4x - 3x \times (3) =$ Now, simplify: $3x \times 4x - 3x \times (3) = 12x^2 - 9x$
Your Turn!	1) $2x(x + 3y) =$ ___	2) $x(x - 7y) =$ ___
	3) $-x(4x - 6y) =$ ___	4) $5x(x + 7y) =$ ___
	5) $-x(3x + 9y) =$ ___	6) $7x(5x - 7y) =$ ___
	7) $-3x(x^3 + 2y^2 - 9x) =$ ___	8) $8x(x^2 - 5y^2 + 7) =$ ___

Topic	Multiplying Monomials
Notes	✓ A monomial is a polynomial with just one term: Examples: $5x$ or $7x^2yz^8$. ✓ When you multiply monomials, first multiply the coefficients (a number placed before and multiplying the variable) and then multiply the variables using multiplication property of exponents. $x^a \times x^b = x^{a+b}$
Example	**Multiply.** $(-5xy^5z^5) \times (2x^2y^4z^6) =$ **Solution:** Multiply coefficients and find same variables and use multiplication property of exponents: $x^a \times x^b = x^{a+b}$ $-5 \times 2 = -10$, $x \times x^2 = x^{1+2} = x^3$, $y^5 \times y^4 = y^{5+4} = y^9$, and $z^5 \times z^6 = z^{5+6} = z^{11}$ Then: $(-5xy^5z^5) \times (2x^2y^4z^6) = -10x^3y^9z^{11}$

Your Turn!

1) $6x^2 \times 3x^4 =$ _____

2) $7x^8 \times 3x^4 =$ _____

3) $-6x^2y^5 \times 7x^3y^6 =$ _____

4) $-4x^7y \times 3x^4y^3 =$ _____

5) $6x^6y^5 \times 5x^3y^4 =$ _____

6) $-5x^6y^5 \times (-9x^8y^4) =$ _____

7) $12x^9y^8z^6 \times 4x^4y^5z =$ _____

8) $-8x^9y^7z^{10} \times 6x^4y^9z^5 =$ _____

Find more at

bit.ly/2KLVoP8

Topic	Factoring Trinomials
Notes	To factor trinomial, use of the following methods: ✓ "FOIL": $(x+a)(x+b) = x^2 + (b+a)x + ab$ ✓ "Difference of Squares": $$a^2 - b^2 = (a+b)(a-b)$$ $$a^2 + 2ab + b^2 = (a+b)(a+b)$$ $$a^2 - 2ab + b^2 = (a-b)(a-b)$$ ✓ "Reverse FOIL": $x^2 + (b+a)x + ab = (x+a)(x+b)$
Example	**Factor this trinomial.** $x^2 + 12x + 35 =$ **Solution:** Break the expression into groups: $(x^2 + 5x) + (7x + 35)$ Now factor out x from $x^2 + 5x$: $x(x+5)$, and factor out 7 from $7x + 35$: $7(x+5)$ Then: $(x^2 + 5x) + (7x + 35) = x(x+5) + 7(x+5)$ Now factor out like term: $(x+5) \rightarrow (x+5)(x+7)$
Your Turn!	1) $x^2 + 4x - 5 =$ ___ 2) $x^2 - x - 6 =$ ___
	3) $x^2 + 4x - 32 =$ ___ 4) $x^2 - 9x + 14 =$ ___
	5) $x^2 + 10x + 24 =$ ___ 6) $x^2 + 17x + 72 =$ ___
	7) $x^2 + 18x + 45 =$ ___ 8) $x^2 - 15x + 56 =$ ___

Find more at

bit.ly/38EpdJA

Chapter 10: Answers

Simplifying Polynomials

1) $-5x + 2$
2) $8x + 18$
3) $8x^2 - 20x$
4) $12x^2 + 42x$
5) $-12x^2$
6) $-47x^2 + 10x$
7) $x^2 + 6x + 5$
8) $x^2 + 14x + 48$
9) $8x^3 + 9x^2$
10) $-3x^5 + 9x^4$

Adding and Subtracting Polynomials

1) $3x^2 - 2x - 5$
2) $8x^3 + 3x - 3$
3) $3x^2 - 7x - 4$
4) $5x^2 - 5$
5) $8x^2 - 1$
6) $x^2 + 8$
7) $8x^3 - 4x$
8) $-5x^4 - 6x$
9) $8x^3 - 1$
10) $-6x^3 + 7x^2 - 4$

Multiplying Binomials

1) $x^2 + 6x + 9$
2) $x^2 + 8x + 15$
3) $x^2 + 4x - 12$
4) $x^2 - 12x + 35$
5) $x^2 + 13x + 36$
6) $x^2 + 14x + 48$
7) $x^2 - 12x + 35$
8) $x^2 - 12x + 36$
9) $x^2 + 5x - 36$
10) $x^2 - 5x - 24$

Multiplying and Dividing Monomials

1) $x^6 y^3$
2) $x^8 y^7$
3) $2x^{11} y^7$
4) $16x^9 y^{10}$
5) $-42x^{11} y^{15}$
6) $-54x^{15} y^7$
7) $6x^2 y^4$
8) $-6x^4 y^9$

Multiplying a Polynomial and a Monomial

1) $2x^2 + 6xy$
2) $x^2 - 7xy$
3) $-4x^2 + 6xy$
4) $5x^2 + 35xy$
5) $-3x^2 - 9xy$
6) $35x^2 - 49xy$
7) $-3x^4 - 6xy^2 + 27x^2$
8) $8x^3 - 40xy^2 + 56x$

Multiplying Monomials

1) $18x^6$
2) $21x^{12}$
3) $-42x^5y^{11}$
4) $-12x^{11}y^4$

5) $30x^9y^9$
6) $45x^{14}y^9$
7) $48x^{13}y^{13}z^7$
8) $-48x^{13}y^{16}z^{15}$

Factoring Trinomials

1) $(x+5)(x-1)$
2) $(x-3)(x+2)$
3) $(x-4)(x+8)$
4) $(x-7)(x-2)$

5) $(x+6)(x+4)$
6) $(x+8)(x+9)$
7) $(x+15)(x+3)$
8) $(x-7)(x-8)$

www.EffortlessMath.com

Chapter 11: Geometry and Solid Figures

Math topics that you'll learn in this chapter:

- ✓ The Pythagorean Theorem
- ✓ Complementary and Supplementary angles
- ✓ Parallel Lines and Transversal
- ✓ Triangles
- ✓ Special Right Triangles
- ✓ Polygons
- ✓ Circles
- ✓ Cubes
- ✓ Trapezoids
- ✓ Rectangle Prisms
- ✓ Cylinder

Topic	**The Pythagorean Theorem**
Notes	✓ In any right triangle: $a^2 + b^2 = c^2$
Example	Right triangle ABC (not shown) has two legs of lengths $9\ cm$ (AB) and $12\ cm$ (AC). What is the length of the third side (BC)? **Solution:** Use Pythagorean Theorem: $a^2 + b^2 = c^2$ Then: $a^2 + b^2 = c^2 \to 9^2 + 12^2 = c^2 \to 81 + 144 = c^2$ $c^2 = 225 \to c = \sqrt{225} = 15\ cm$
Your Turn! **Find more at** bit.ly/37Jl08v	1) _____ (triangle with legs 4 and 3, hypotenuse ?) 2) _____ (triangle with hypotenuse 20, leg 16, other leg ?) 3) _____ (triangle with hypotenuse 15, leg 9, other leg ?) 4) _____ (triangle with hypotenuse 13, leg 12, other leg ?)

Topic	Complementary and Supplementary Angles
Notes	✓ Complementary angles are two angles with a sum of $90°$. A common case is when they form a right angle. ✓ Supplementary angles are two angles with a sum of $180°$. A common case is when they lie on the same side of a straight line.
Example	**Find the missing angle.** **Solution:** Notice that two angles form a straight angle when together. This means that the angles are supplementary and have a sum of $180°$. $x + 43 = 180 \rightarrow x = 180 - 43 = 137°$
Your Turn!	**Find the missing measurement in the pair of angles.** 1) $x =$ ___ 2) $x =$ ___

Find more at

bit.ly/3nlOn6G

Topic	Parallel lines and Transversals
Notes	✓ When a line (transversal) intersects two parallel lines in the same plane, eight angles are formed. In the following diagram, a transversal intersects two parallel lines. Angles 1, 7, 3, and 5 are congruent. Angles 2, 8, 4, and 6 are also congruent. ✓ In the following diagram, the following angles are supplementary angles (their sum is 180): - Angles 1 and 8 - Angles 2 and 7 - Angles 3 and 6 - Angles 4 and 5
Example	**In the following diagram, two parallel lines are cut by a transversal. What is the value of** x**?** **Solution:** The two angles $75°$ and $11x - 2$ are equal. $11x - 2 = 75$ Now, solve for x: $11x - 2 + 2 = 75 + 2 \rightarrow$ $11x = 77 \rightarrow x = \dfrac{77}{11} \rightarrow x = 7$
Your Turn!	1) Find the measure of the angle indicated. ? = ___ $100°$? 2) Solve for x. $x =$ ___ $x + 139$ $132°$

Topic	Triangles
Notes	✓ In any triangle the sum of all angles is 180 degrees. ✓ Area of a triangle = $\frac{1}{2}(base \times height)$
Example	**What is the area of the following triangle?** Solution: Use the area formula: Area = $\frac{1}{2}(base \times height)$ $base = 12$ and $height = 8$ Area = $\frac{1}{2}(12 \times 8) = \frac{96}{2} = 48$

Your Turn!

1) _____ (right triangle with legs 10 and 5)

2) _____ (right triangle with legs 12 and 16)

3) _____ (right triangle with legs 22 and 30)

4) _____ (right triangle with legs 32 and 40)

Geometry and Solid Figures

Topic	Special Right Triangles
Notes	✓ A special right triangle is a triangle whose sides are in a particular ratio. Two special right triangles are $45° - 45° - 90°$ and $30° - 60° - 90°$ triangles. ✓ In a special $45° - 45° - 90°$ triangle, the three angles are $45°$, $45°$ and $90°$. The lengths of the sides of this triangle are in the ratio of $1 : 1 : \sqrt{2}$. ✓ In a special triangle $30° - 60° - 90°$, the three angles are $30° - 60° - 90°$. The lengths of this triangle are in the ratio of $1 : \sqrt{3} : 2$.
Example	*Find the length of the hypotenuse of a right triangle if the length of the other two sides are both* 5 *inches.* ***Solution:*** this is a right triangle with two equal sides. Therefore, it must be a $45° - 45° - 90°$ triangle. Two equal sides are 5 inches. So, the length of the hypotenuse is $5\sqrt{2}$ inches. If the first and second value of the ratio x: x: x$\sqrt{2}$. $$x : x : x\sqrt{2} \rightarrow x = 5 \rightarrow 5 : 5 : 5\sqrt{2}$$
Your Turn!	*Find the value of x and y in each triangle.* 1) $x = $ ___ $y = $ ___ 2) $x = $ ___ $y = $ ___

Find more at

bit.ly/3xL9bJR

Topic	**Polygons**
Notes	Perimeter of a square = 4 × side = 4s Perimeter of a rectangle = 2(width + length) Perimeter of trapezoid = a + b + c + d Perimeter of a regular hexagon = 6a Perimeter of a parallelogram = 2(l + w)
Example	*Find the perimeter of following regular hexagon.* **Solution:** Since the hexagon is regular, all sides are equal. Then: Perimeter of Hexagon = 6 × (one side) Perimeter of Hexagon = 6 × (one side) = 6 × 7 = 42 m
Your Turn!	1) *(rectangle)* _____ 7 in, 13 in 2) *(trapezoid)* _____ 7 m, 9 m, 9 m, 12 m 3) *(regular hexagon)* ____ 8 m 4) *(parallelogram)* _____ 8 in, 14 in

Geometry and Solid Figures

Topic	Circles
Notes	✓ In a circle, variable r is usually used for the radius and d for diameter and π is about 3.14. ✓ Area of a circle $= \pi r^2$ ✓ Circumference of a circle $= 2\pi r$
Example	**Find the area of the circle.** **Solution:** Use area formula: $Area = \pi r^2$ $r = 3\ in \rightarrow Area = \pi(3)^2 = 9\pi, \pi = 3.14$ **Then:** $Area = 9 \times 3.14 = 28.26\ in^2$
Your Turn!	**Find the area of each circle.** ($\pi = 3.14$) 1) ____ (4 cm) 2) ____ (12 in) **Find the Circumference of each circle.** ($\pi = 3.14$) 3) ____ (6 cm) 4) ____ (11 m)

Find more at
bit.ly/3nJdOP2

Topic	Cubes
Notes	✓ A cube is a three-dimensional solid object bounded by six square sides. ✓ Volume is the measure of the amount of space inside of a solid figure, like a cube, ball, cylinder or pyramid. ✓ Volume of a cube = $(one\ side)^3$ ✓ surface area of cube = $6 \times (one\ side)^2$
Example	**Find the volume and surface area of the following cube.** 15 cm **Solution:** Use volume formula: $volume = (one\ side)^3$ Then: $volume = (one\ side)^3 = (15)^3 = 3,375\ cm^3$ Use surface area formula: $surface\ area\ of\ cube$: $6(one\ side)^2 = 6(15)^2 = 6(225) = 1,350\ cm^2$
Your Turn!	**Find the volume of each cube.** 1) _____ 8 in 2) _____ 11 ft 3) _____ 15 cm 4) _____ 22 m

Find more at

bit.ly/2M6PfOI

Geometry and Solid Figures

Topic	Trapezoids
Notes	✓ A quadrilateral with at least one pair of parallel sides is a trapezoid. ✓ Area of a trapezoid $= \frac{1}{2}h(b_1 + b_2)$
Example	**Calculate the area of the trapezoid.** Solution: Use area formula: $A = \frac{1}{2}h(b_1 + b_2)$ $b_1 = 8\ cm$, $b_2 = 12\ cm$ and $h = 14\ cm$ Then: $A = \frac{1}{2}(14)(12 + 8) = 7(20) = 140\ cm^2$
Your Turn!	1) _____ (6 cm, 4 cm, 10 cm) 2) _____ (9 m, 10 m, 12 m) 3) _____ (8 ft, 6 ft, 16 ft) 4) _____ (9 cm, 6 cm, 14 cm)

Find more at
bit.ly/3hpKACJ

Topic	**Rectangular Prisms**
Notes	✓ A solid 3-dimensional object which has six rectangular faces. ✓ Volume of a Rectangular prism = $Length \times Width \times Height$ $Volume = l \times w \times h$ $Surface\ area = 2(wh + lw + lh)$
Example	**Find the volume and surface area of rectangular prism.** **Solution:** Use volume formula: $Volume = l \times w \times h$ Then: $Volume = 4 \times 2 \times 6 = 48\ m^3$ Use surface area formula: $Surface\ area = 2(wh + lw + lh)$ Then: $Surface\ area = 2((2 \times 6) + (4 \times 2) + (4 \times 6))$ $= 2(12 + 8 + 24) = 2(44) = 88\ m^2$
Your Turn!	**Find the surface area of each Rectangular Prism.** 1) _____ (5 ft, 8 ft, 3 ft) 2) _____ (7 cm, 14 cm, 6 cm) 3) _____ (10 m, 15 m, 10 m) 4) _____ (16 in, 14 in, 12 in)

Find more at

bit.ly/3nKm2GT

Geometry and Solid Figures

Topic	Cylinder
Notes	✓ A cylinder is a solid geometric figure with straight parallel sides and a circular or oval cross section. ✓ Volume of Cylinder Formula $= \pi(radius)^2 \times height$ $\pi = 3.14$ ✓ Surface area of a cylinder $= 2\pi r^2 + 2\pi rh$
Example	**Find the volume and Surface area of the follow Cylinder.** Solution: Use volume formula: $Volume = \pi(radius)^2 \times height$ Then: $Volume = \pi(4)^2 \times 10 = 16\pi \times 10 = 160\pi$ $\pi = 3.14$ **then:** $Volume = 160\pi = 502.4 \ cm^3$ Use surface area formula: $Surface\ area = 2\pi r^2 + 2\pi rh$ **Then:** $2\pi(4)^2 + 2\pi(4)(10) = 2\pi(16) + 2\pi(40) = 32\pi + 80\pi = 112\pi$ $\pi = 3.14$ **Then:** $Surface\ area = 112 \times 3.14 = 351.68\ cm^2$
Your Turn!	**Find the volume of each Cylinder.** ($\pi = 3.14$) 1) _____ (7 in, 3 in) 2) _____ (11 m, 6 m) **Find the Surface area of each Cylinder.** ($\pi = 3.14$) 3) _____ (12 ft, 9 ft) 4) _____ (14 cm, 7 cm)

Find more at

bit.ly/37LtcVM

Chapter 11: Answers

The Pythagorean Theorem

1) 5
2) 12
3) 12
4) 5

Complementary and Supplementary Angles

1) 66°
2) 35°

Parallel lines and Transversals

1) 80°
2) −7

Triangles

1) 25
2) 96
3) 330
4) 640

Special Right Triangles

1) $x = 24$ $y = 12\sqrt{3}$
2) $x = 7$ $y = 7\sqrt{2}$

Polygons

1) 40 in
2) 37 m
3) 48 m
4) 44 in

Circles

1) 50.24 cm^2
2) 452.16 in^2
3) 37.68 cm
4) 69.08 m

Cubes

1) 512 in^3
2) 1,331 ft^3
3) 3,375 cm^3
4) 10,648 m^3

Trapezoids

1) 32 cm^2
2) 105 m^2
3) 72 ft^2
4) 69 cm^2

Rectangle Prisms

1) $158 \, ft^2$
2) $448 \, cm^2$
3) $800 \, m^2$
4) $1,168 \, in^2$

Cylinder

1) $197.82 \, in^3$
2) $1,243.44 \, m^3$
3) $1,186.92 \, ft^2$
4) $923.16 \, cm^2$

Chapter 12 Statistics

Math topics that you'll learn in this chapter:

- ✓ Mean, Median, Mode, and Range of the Given Data
- ✓ Probability Problems
- ✓ Pie Graph
- ✓ Permutations and Combinations

Topic	Mean, Median, Mode, and Range of the Given Data
Notes	✓ Mean: $\dfrac{sum\ of\ the\ data}{total\ number\ of\ data\ entires}$ ✓ Mode: value in the list that appears most often. ✓ Median: is the middle number of a group of numbers that have been arranged in order by size. ✓ Range: the difference of largest value and smallest value in the list.
Example	**Find the mode and median of these numbers?** 18, 11, 6, 3, 1, 18, 2, 8 **Solution:** Mode: value in the list that appears most often. Number 18 is the value in the list that appears most often (there are two number 18). To find median, write the numbers in order: 1, 2, 3, 6, 8, 11, 18, 18 Number 6 and 8 are in the middle. Find their average: $\dfrac{6+8}{2} = \dfrac{14}{2} = 7$ The median is 7.

Your Turn!

1) 7, 6, 3, 8, 7, 5

Mode: _____   Range: _____

Mean: _____   Median: _____

2) 6, 3, 2, 12, 8, 6, 5, 14

Mode: _____   Range: _____

Mean: _____   Median: _____

3) 4, 9, 3, 1, 5, 4, 18, 12

Mode: _____   Range: _____

Mean: _____   Median: _____

4) 12, 9, 8, 5, 9, 7, 4, 10

Mode: _____   Range: _____

Mean: _____   Median: _____

Find more at

bit.ly/2KO86gg

Topic	Probability Problems
Notes	✓ Probability is the likelihood of something happening in the future. It is expressed as a number between zero (can never happen) to 1 (will always happen). ✓ Probability can be expressed as a fraction, a decimal, or a percent. ✓ Probability formula: $Probability = \frac{number\ of\ desired\ outcomes}{number\ of\ total\ outcomes}$
Example	***If there are 3 green balls, 4 red balls, and 10 blue balls in a basket, what is the probability that Jason will pick out a red ball from the basket?*** **Solution:** There are 4 red ball and 17 are total number of balls. Therefore, probability that Jason will pick out a red ball from the basket is 4 out of 17 or $\frac{4}{3+4+10} = \frac{4}{17}$
Your Turn!	1) A number is chosen at random from 1 to 12. Find the probability of selecting a prime number. (A prime number is a whole number that is only divisible by itself and 1) _____
	2) There are only red and blue cards in a box. The probability of choosing a red card in the box at random is one third. If there are 32 blue cards, how many cards are in the box? _____
Find more at bit.ly/3phwk1p	3) A die is rolled, what is the probability that an even number is obtained? _____

Topic	**Pie Graph**
Notes	✓ A Pie Chart is a circle chart divided into sectors; each sector represents the relative size of each value.
Example	A library has 420 books that include Mathematics, Physics, Chemistry, English and History. Use following graph to answer the question. **What is the number of Physics books?** **Solution:** Number of total books = 420 Percent of Physics books = 25% = 0.25 Then, umber of Physics books: $$0.25 \times 420 = 105$$
Your Turn!	The circle graph below shows all Mr. Smith's expenses for last month. Mr. Smith spent $520 for clothes last month. Mr. Smith's last month expenses
Find more at bit.ly/34ECTDv	1) How much did Mr. Smith spend for his Books last month? _____ 2) How much did Mr. Smith spend for Bills last month? _____ 3) How much did Mr. Smith spend for his foods last month? _____

Topic	**Permutations and Combinations**
Notes	✓ Permutations: The number of ways to choose a sample of k elements from a set of n distinct objects where order does matter, and replacements are not allowed. For a permutation problem, use this formula: $$_nP_k = \frac{n!}{(n-k)!}$$ ✓ Combination: The number of ways to choose a sample of r elements from a set of n distinct objects where order does not matter, and replacements are not allowed. For a combination problem, use this formula: $$_nC_r = \frac{n!}{r!\,(n-r)!}$$ ✓ Factorials are products, indicated by an exclamation mark. For example, 4! Equals: $4 \times 3 \times 2 \times 1$. Remember that 0! is defined to be equal to 1.
Example	*How many ways can we pick a team of 5 people from a group of 8?* **Solution:** Since the order doesn't matter, we need to use combination formula where n is 8 and r is 5. Then: $\frac{n!}{r!\,(n-r)!} = \frac{8!}{5!\,(8-5)!} = \frac{8!}{5!\,(3)!} = \frac{8 \times 7 \times 6 \times 5!}{5!\,(3)!} = \frac{8 \times 7 \times 6}{3 \times 2 \times 1} = \frac{56}{2} = 28$
Your Turn! **Find more at** bit.ly/34BQgUY	1) In how many ways can 7 athletes be arranged in a straight line? _____ 2) How many ways can we award a first and second place prize among seven contestants? _____ 3) In how many ways can we choose 3 players from a team of 9 players? _____

Chapter 12: Answers

Mean, Median, Mode, and Range of the Given data

1) Mode: 7   Range: 5   Mean: 6   Median: 6.5
2) Mode: 6   Range: 12   Mean: 7   Median: 6
3) Mode: 4   Range: 17   Mean: 7   Median: 4.5
4) Mode: 9   Range: 8   Mean: 8   Median: 8.5

Probability Problems

1) $\frac{5}{12}$ 2) 48   3) $\frac{1}{2}$

Pie Graph

1) $312   2) $520   3) $650

Permutations and Combinations

1) 5,040   2) 42   3) 84

CHAPTER 13: Functions Operations

Math topics that you'll learn in this chapter:

- ✓ Function Notation and Evaluation
- ✓ Adding and Subtracting Functions
- ✓ Multiplying and Dividing Functions
- ✓ Composition of Functions

Functions Operations

Topic	Function Notation and Evaluation
Notes	✓ Functions are mathematical operations that assign unique outputs to given inputs. ✓ Function notation is the way a function is written. It is meant to be a precise way of giving information about the function without a rather lengthy written explanation. ✓ The most popular function notation is $f(x)$ which is read "f of x". ✓ To evaluate a function, plug in the input (the given value or expression) for the function's variable (place holder, x).
Example	**Evaluate**: $h(n) = n^2 - 3$, find $h(4)$. **Solution**: Substitute n with 4: Then: $h(n) = n^2 - 3 \rightarrow h(4) = (4)^2 - 3 = 16 - 3 \rightarrow h(4) = 13$

Your Turn!

1) $f(x) = x - 5$, find $f(-4)$ _____

2) $g(x) = 4x + 2$, find $g(3)$ _____

3) $g(n) = 6n - 4$, find $g(-2)$ _____

4) $h(n) = n^2 - 8$, find $h(-5)$ _____

5) $f(x) = x^2 + 9$, find $f(-4)$ _____

6) $g(x) = 3x^2 - 7$, find $g(-6)$ _____

7) $w(x) = 4x^2 - x$, find $w(3n)$ _____

8) $p(x) = 3x^3 - 7$, find $p(-2a)$ _____

Find more at bit.ly/3mls7lF

Topic	Adding and Subtracting Functions
Notes	✓ Just like we can add and subtract numbers and expressions, we can add or subtract two functions and simplify or evaluate them. The result is a new function. ✓ For two functions $f(x)$ and $g(x)$, we can create two new functions: $(f+g)(x) = f(x) + g(x)$ and $(f-g)(x) = f(x) - g(x)$
Example	$g(a) = 3a - 2, f(a) = a + 5$, **Find:** $(g + f)(a)$ **Solution:** $(g + f)(a) = g(a) + f(a)$ Then: $(g + f)(a) = (3a - 2) + (a + 5) = 4a + 3$
Your Turn!	1) $g(x) = x - 6$ $h(x) = 2x + 4$ Find: $(h + g)(3)$ _____ 3) $f(x) = 4x + 9$ $g(x) = 3x - 10$ Find: $(f - g)(-4)$ _____ 5) $g(x) = 9x - 7$ $h(x) = 6x^2 + 10$ Find: $(h - g)(x)$ _____	2) $f(x) = 3x + 4$ $g(x) = -x - 8$ Find: $(f + g)(2)$ _____ 4) $h(x) = 4x^2 - 6$ $g(x) = 2x + 11$ Find: $(h + g)(5)$ _____ 6) $h(x) = -2x^2 - 18$ $g(x) = 3x^2 + 10$ Find: $(h - g)(a)$ _____

Find more at
bit.ly/3hdeFVO

Topic	Multiplying and Dividing Functions
Notes	✓ Just like we can multiply and divide numbers and expressions, we can multiply and divide two functions and simplify or evaluate them. ✓ For two functions $f(x)$ and $g(x)$, we can create two new functions: $$(f \cdot g)(x) = f(x) \cdot g(x) \text{ and } \left(\frac{f}{g}\right)(x) = \frac{f(x)}{g(x)}$$
Example	$g(x) = x + 9, f(x) = x - 2$, Find: $(g \cdot f)(3)$ **Solution:** $(g \cdot f)(x) = g(x) \cdot f(x) = (x+9)(x-2) = x^2 - 2x + 9x - 18 = x^2 + 7x - 18$ Substitute x with 3: $(g \cdot f)(x) = (3)^2 + 7(3) - 18 = 9 + 21 - 18 = 12$

Your Turn!

1) $g(x) = x - 5$
   $h(x) = x + 3$
   Find: $(g \cdot h)(4)$
   _____

2) $f(x) = x + 6$
   $g(x) = -x - 6$
   Find: $\left(\frac{f}{g}\right)(-2)$
   _____

3) $f(x) = 3x + 6$
   $g(x) = 2x - 7$
   Find: $\left(\frac{f}{g}\right)(4)$
   _____

4) $h(x) = x^2 - 8$
   $g(x) = x + 4$
   Find: $(g \cdot h)(-3)$
   _____

5) $g(x) = 5x - 9$
   $h(x) = x^2 - 6$
   Find: $(g \cdot h)(-3)$
   _____

6) $h(x) = 4x^2 - 7$
   $g(x) = -3x - 9$
   Find: $\left(\frac{h}{g}\right)(-2)$
   _____

Find more at
bit.ly/3ph7kHA

Topic	Composition of Functions
Notes	✓ "Composition of functions" simply means combining two or more functions in a way where the output from one function becomes the input for the next function. ✓ The notation used for composition is: $(fog)(x) = f(g(x))$ and is read "f composed with g of x" or "f of g of x".
Example	**Using $f(x) = x - 4$ and $g(x) = x + 1$, find: $(fog)(4)$** **Solution:** $(fog)(x) = f(g(x))$ Then: $(fog)(x) = f(g(x)) = f(x + 1) = x + 1 - 4 = x - 3$ Substitute x with 4: $(fog)(4) = f(g(4)) = 4 - 3 = 1$
Your Turn!	1) $f(x) = 2x$ $g(x) = x + 3$ Find: $(fog)(2)$ _____ 2) $f(x) = x + 5$ $g(x) = x - 7$ Find: $(fog)(-2)$ _____
	3) $f(x) = 4x$ $g(x) = x + 5$ Find: $(gof)(4)$ _____ 4) $h(x) = x - 2$ $g(x) = 3x + 4$ Find: $(goh)(2)$ _____
	5) $f(x) = 4x - 2$ $g(x) = x + 9$ Find: $(fog)(-1)$ _____ 6) $f(x) = x^2 - 3$ $g(x) = 3x - 5$ Find: $(gof)(2)$ _____

Find more at

bit.ly/2WHBkAg

Chapter 13: Answers

Function Notation and Evaluation

1) -9
2) 14
3) -16
4) 17
5) 25
6) 101
7) $36n^2 - 3n$
8) $-24a^3 - 7$

Adding and Subtracting Functions

1) 7
2) 0
3) 15
4) 115
5) $6x^2 - 9x + 17$
6) $-5a^2 - 28$

Multiplying and Dividing Function

1) -7
2) -1
3) 18
4) 1
5) -72
6) -3

Composition of Function

1) 10
2) -4
3) 21
4) 4
5) 30
6) -2

Time to Test

Time to refine your Math skills with a practice test

In this section, there are two complete TSI Mathematics Tests. Take these tests to simulate the test day experience. After you've finished, score your test using the answer keys.

Before You Start

- You'll need a pencil and a calculator to take the test.
- For each question, there are four possible answers. Choose which one is best.
- It's okay to guess. There is no penalty for wrong answers.
- After you've finished the test, review the answer key to see where you went wrong.

Good Luck!

TSIA2 Mathematics Practice Test 1
2023-2024

Total number of questions: 20

Total time: No time limit

You may use a calculator on this Test.

TSI Math Practice Test Answer Sheet

Remove (or photocopy) this answer sheet and use it to complete the practice test.

TSI Math Practice Test 1 Answer Sheet

1	Ⓐ Ⓑ Ⓒ Ⓓ	16	Ⓐ Ⓑ Ⓒ Ⓓ
2	Ⓐ Ⓑ Ⓒ Ⓓ	17	Ⓐ Ⓑ Ⓒ Ⓓ
3	Ⓐ Ⓑ Ⓒ Ⓓ	18	Ⓐ Ⓑ Ⓒ Ⓓ
4	Ⓐ Ⓑ Ⓒ Ⓓ	19	Ⓐ Ⓑ Ⓒ Ⓓ
5	Ⓐ Ⓑ Ⓒ Ⓓ	20	Ⓐ Ⓑ Ⓒ Ⓓ
6	Ⓐ Ⓑ Ⓒ Ⓓ		
7	Ⓐ Ⓑ Ⓒ Ⓓ		
8	Ⓐ Ⓑ Ⓒ Ⓓ		
9	Ⓐ Ⓑ Ⓒ Ⓓ		
10	Ⓐ Ⓑ Ⓒ Ⓓ		
11	Ⓐ Ⓑ Ⓒ Ⓓ		
12	Ⓐ Ⓑ Ⓒ Ⓓ		
13	Ⓐ Ⓑ Ⓒ Ⓓ		
14	Ⓐ Ⓑ Ⓒ Ⓓ		
15	Ⓐ Ⓑ Ⓒ Ⓓ		

www.EffortlessMath.com

1) 38 is What percent of 50?

   A. 45%

   B. 52%

   C. 64%

   D. 76%

2) A rectangle has 14 cm wide and 5 cm length. What is the perimeter of this rectangle?

   A. 38 cm

   B. 43 cm

   C. 49 cm

   D. 58 cm

3) What is the product of all possible values of x in the following equation?

$$|x - 10| = 3$$

   A. 7

   B. 13

   C. 80

   D. 91

4) What is the value of the following expression? $3\frac{1}{4} + 2\frac{4}{16} + 1\frac{3}{8} + 5\frac{1}{2}$

   A. $3\frac{10}{14}$

   B. $4\frac{1}{2}$

   C. $12\frac{4}{16}$

   D. $12\frac{3}{8}$

5) A certain insect has a mass of 85 milligrams. What is the insect's mass in grams?

   A. 0.08

   B. 0.085

   C. 0.85

   D. 85

6) If $m = 6$ and $n = -3$, what is the value of $\frac{5-9(3+n)}{3m-5(2-n)} = ?$

A. $-\frac{4}{7}$

B. $-\frac{5}{7}$

C. $\frac{3}{7}$

D. $\frac{2}{7}$

7) Clara has 28 cookies. She is inviting 7 friends to a party. How many cookies will each friends get?

A. 2

B. 4

C. 7

D. 8

8) How long will it take to receive $360 in investment of $240 at the rate of 10% simple interest?

A. 9 years

B. 15 years

C. 18 years

D. 21 years

9) How many hours are there in 1,800 minutes?

A. 20 hours

B. 25 hours

C. 30 hours

D. 33 hours

10) A shoes originally priced at $45.00 was on sale for 15% off. Nick received a 20% employee discount applied to the sale price. How much did Nick pay for the shoes?

A. $30.60

B. $34.50

C. $37.30

D. $42.25

11) In a class, there are 18 boys and 12 girls. What is the ratio of the number of boys to number of girls?

   A. 1 : 2

   B. 2 : 3

   C. 1 : 3

   D. 3 : 2

12) The shaded sector of the circle shown below has an area of 12π square feet. What is the circumference of the circle?

   A. 24π feet

   B. 81π feet

   C. 124π feet

   D. 180π feet

13) Which of the following is a factor of 45?

   A. 7

   B. 9

   C. 11

   D. 13

14) By what percent did the price of a shirt increase if its price was increased from $15.30 to $18.36?

   A. 10%

   B. 12%

   C. 16%

   D. 20%

15) The greatest common factor of 32 and x is 8. How many possible values for x are greater than 10 and less than 60?

   A. 1

   B. 4

   C. 6

   D. 7

16) A box contains 6 strawberry candies, 4 orange candies, and 3 banana candies. If Roberto selects 2 candies at random from this box, without replacement, what is the probability that both candies are not orange?

   A. $\frac{1}{8}$

   B. $\frac{2}{13}$

   C. $\frac{6}{13}$

   D. $\frac{1}{28}$

17) $100(3 + 0.1)^2 - 100 = \cdots$

   A. 861

   B. 865.5

   C. 1,000

   D. 1,000.3

18) How many integers are between $\frac{7}{2}$ and $\frac{30}{4}$?

   A. 3

   B. 4

   C. 6

   D. 10

19) In a certain state, the sales tax rate increased from 8% to 8.5%. What was the increase in the sales tax on a $250 item?

   A. $1.00

   B. $1.25

   C. $1.90

   D. $2.30

20) $(4m + 8) - (6 - 8m) = \cdots$

   A. $12m + 2$

   B. $10 + 2$

   C. $8m - 2$

   D. $6m + 2$

End of TSI Mathematics Practice Test 1 **STOP**

TSIA2 Mathematics Practice Test 2

2023 - 2024

Total number of questions: 20

Total time: No time limit

You may use a calculator on this Test.

TSI Math Practice Test Answer Sheet

Remove (or photocopy) this answer sheet and use it to complete the practice test.

TSI Math Practice Test 2 Answer Sheet

1 Ⓐ Ⓑ Ⓒ Ⓓ		16 Ⓐ Ⓑ Ⓒ Ⓓ	
2 Ⓐ Ⓑ Ⓒ Ⓓ		17 Ⓐ Ⓑ Ⓒ Ⓓ	
3 Ⓐ Ⓑ Ⓒ Ⓓ		18 Ⓐ Ⓑ Ⓒ Ⓓ	
4 Ⓐ Ⓑ Ⓒ Ⓓ		19 Ⓐ Ⓑ Ⓒ Ⓓ	
5 Ⓐ Ⓑ Ⓒ Ⓓ		20 Ⓐ Ⓑ Ⓒ Ⓓ	
6 Ⓐ Ⓑ Ⓒ Ⓓ			
7 Ⓐ Ⓑ Ⓒ Ⓓ			
8 Ⓐ Ⓑ Ⓒ Ⓓ			
9 Ⓐ Ⓑ Ⓒ Ⓓ			
10 Ⓐ Ⓑ Ⓒ Ⓓ			
11 Ⓐ Ⓑ Ⓒ Ⓓ			
12 Ⓐ Ⓑ Ⓒ Ⓓ			
13 Ⓐ Ⓑ Ⓒ Ⓓ			
14 Ⓐ Ⓑ Ⓒ Ⓓ			
15 Ⓐ Ⓑ Ⓒ Ⓓ			

1) In a scale diagram, 0.15 inch represents 150 feet. How many inches represent 2.5 feet?

   A. 0.001 in

   B. 0.012 in

   C. 0.0025 in

   D. 0.002 in

2) If $\frac{3}{7}$ of Z is 54, what is $\frac{2}{5}$ of Z?

   A. 44.2

   B. 46.3

   C. 48.4

   D. 50.4

3) Mary has 8 blue pens, 2 green pens, and 4 black pens. If she picks out one pen randomly, what is the probability that she picks a blue pen?

   A. $\frac{3}{7}$

   B. $\frac{4}{7}$

   C. $\frac{5}{7}$

   D. $\frac{6}{7}$

4) A car travels at a speed of 72 miles per hour. How far will it travel in 8 hours?

   A. 574 miles

   B. 576 miles

   C. 578 miles

   D. 580 miles

5) If Sam spent $60 on sweets and he spent 25% of the selling price for the tip, how much did he spend?

   A. $66

   B. $69

   C. $72

   D. $75

6) Which of the following numbers has factors that include the smallest factor (other than 1) of 95?

   A. 28

   B. 32

   C. 39

   D. 45

7) $\frac{4^2+3^2+(-5)^2}{(9+10-11)^2} =$

   A. $\frac{25}{32}$

   B. 56

   C. -56

   D. $-\frac{25}{32}$

8) Angle A and angle B are supplementary. The measure of angle A is 2 times the measure of angle B. What is the measure of angle A in degrees?

   A. $100°$

   B. $120°$

   C. $140°$

   D. $160°$

9) $200(3 + 0.01)^2 - 200 =$

   A. 201.55

   B. 361.08

   C. 702.88

   D. 1,612.02

10) If $x = -2$ in the following equation, what is the value of y? $2x + 3 = \frac{y+6}{5}$

    A. -9

    B. -11

    C. -13

    D. -15

11) Tomas is 6 feet 8.5 inches tall, and Alex is 5 feet 3 inches tall. What is the difference in height, in inches, between Alex and Tomas?

   A. 2.5

   B. 7.5

   C. 12.5

   D. 17.5

12) What is the solution to $\frac{0.02}{0.25} = \frac{1.25}{x}$?

   A. 0.150

   B. 1.156

   C. 11.565

   D. 15.625

13) The least of 8 consecutive integers is m, and the greatest is n. What is the value of $\frac{m+n}{3}$ in terms of m?

   A. $m + 1$

   B. $2m + 8$

   C. $\frac{2m+7}{3}$

   D. $\frac{2m}{7}$

14) In the infinitely repeating decimal below, 1 is the first digit in the repeating pattern. What is the 68th digit? $\frac{1}{7} = 0.\overline{142857}$

   A. 1

   B. 2

   C. 4

   D. 7

15) Yesterday Kylie writes 10% of her homework. Today she writes another 18% of the entire homework. What fraction of the homework is left for her to write?

A. $\frac{7}{25}$

B. $\frac{4}{25}$

C. $\frac{18}{25}$

D. $\frac{10}{25}$

16) In a box of blue and yellow pens, the ratio of yellow pens to blue pens is $2:3$. If the box contains 9 blue pens, how many yellow pens are there?

A. 3

B. 4

C. 5

D. 6

17) What decimal is equivalent to $-\frac{6}{9}$?

A. $-0.\overline{5}$

B. $-0.\overline{6}$

C. $-0.\overline{65}$

D. $-0.\overline{7}$

18) How many positive even factors of 68 are greater than 26 and less than 60?

A. 0

B. 1

C. 2

D. 6

19) Simplify: $-11.6 + 6.7 - 2(-15.3)$

A. 19.7

B. 21.7

C. 23.7

D. 25.7

20) The ratio of two sides of a parallelogram is 2: 3. If its perimeter is 40 cm, find the length of its sides.

A. 8 cm, 12 cm

B. 10 cm, 14 cm

C. 12 cm, 16 cm

D. 14 cm, 18 cm

End of TSI Mathematics Practice Test 2 STOP

TSI Mathematics Practice Test Answers

Now, it's time to review your results to see where you went wrong and what areas you need to improve!

TSI Math Practice Test 1		TSI Math Practice Test 2	
1	D	1	C
2	A	2	D
3	D	3	B
4	D	4	B
5	B	5	D
6	B	6	D
7	B	7	A
8	B	8	B
9	C	9	D
10	A	10	B
11	D	11	D
12	A	12	D
13	B	13	C
14	D	14	C
15	B	15	C
16	C	16	D
17	A	17	B
18	B	18	B
19	B	19	D
20	A	20	A

TSI Mathematics Practice Test Answers and Explanations

TSI Mathematics Practice Test 1

1) Choice D is correct

$\frac{38}{50} = 0.76$, converting 0.76 to percent we have: $0.76 = 76\%$. Then, 38 is 76% of 50.

2) Choice A is correct

Perimeter of rectangle is equal to the sum of all the sides of the rectangle:

Perimeter $= 2(14) + 2(5) = 28 + 10 = 38 \; cm$

3) Choice D is correct

To solve absolute values equations, write two equations. $x - 10$ could be positive 3, or negative 3. Therefore, $x - 10 = 3 \Rightarrow x = 13$

$x - 10 = -3 \Rightarrow x = 7$. Find the product of the solutions: $7 \times 13 = 91$

4) Choice D is correct

$3\frac{1}{4} + 2\frac{4}{16} + 1\frac{3}{8} + 5\frac{1}{2}$

Convert all the fractions to a common denominator (16):

$3\frac{4}{16} + 2\frac{4}{16} + 1\frac{6}{16} + 5\frac{8}{16} = (3 + 2 + 1 + 5) + \left(\frac{4+4+6+8}{16}\right) = 11 + 1\frac{6}{16} = 12\frac{6}{16} = 12\frac{3}{8}$

5) Choice B is correct

One gram is equal to 1,000 milligrams, or 1 milligram is equal to $\frac{1}{1,000}$ gram

Thus, 85 milligrams $= \frac{85}{1,000} = 0.085$ gram

6) Choice B is correct

Substitute 6 for m and -3 for n:

$\frac{5-9(3+n)}{3m-5(2-n)} = \frac{5-9(3+(-3))}{3(6)-5(2-(-3))} = \frac{5-9(0)}{18-5(5)} = \frac{5}{18-25} = \frac{5}{-7} = -\frac{5}{7}$

7) Choice B is correct

To answer this question, we need to divide 28 by 7: $\frac{28}{7} = 4$

8) Choice B is correct

Simple interest (y) is calculated by multiplying the initial deposit (p), by the interest rate (r), and time (t). $360 = 240 \times 0.10 \times t \rightarrow 360 = 24t \rightarrow t = \frac{360}{24} = 15$

So, it takes 15 years to get \$360 with an investment of \$240.

9) Choice C is correct

There are 60 minutes in 1 hours. Divide the number of minutes by the number of minutes in 1 hour: $\frac{1,800}{60} = 30$ hours

10) Choice A is correct

First, find the sale price. 15% of \$45.00 is \$6.75, so the sale price is $\$45.00 - \$6.75 = \$38.25$. Next, find the price after Nick's employee discount. $20\% \times \$38.25 = \$7.65$, so, the final price of the shoes is $\$38.25 - \$7.65 = \$30.60$

11) Choice D is correct

Write the numbers in the ratio and simplify: $18:12 \rightarrow 3:2$

12) Choice A is correct

The area of the entire circle is πr^2. The fraction of the circle that is shaded is $\frac{30}{360} = \frac{1}{12}$. So, the area of the sector is $\frac{1}{12}\pi r^2$. Use that information to find r.

$\frac{1}{12}\pi r^2 = 12\pi \rightarrow r^2 = 144 \rightarrow r = 12$

Use r to calculate the circumference of the circle: $c = 2\pi r = 2\pi(12) = 24\pi$

The circumference is 24π feet.

13) Choice B is correct

The factors of 45 are: $\{1, 3, 5, 9, 15, 45\}$. Only choice B is correct.

14) Choice D is correct.

$Percent\ of\ change = \frac{new\ number - original\ number}{original\ number} = \frac{18.36 - 15.30}{15.30} = 20\%$

15) Choice B is correct

First find the multiples of 8 that fall between 10 and 60: 16, 24, 32, 40, 48, 56. Since the greatest common factor of 32 and x is 8, x cannot be 32 (otherwise the GCF would be 32, not 8). There are 5 remaining values: 16, 24, 40, 48 and 56. Number 16 is also not possible (otherwise the GCF would be 16, not 8). Then, there are 4 possible values for x.

16) Choice C is correct

The total number of candies in the box is $6 + 4 + 3 = 13$. The number of candies that are not orange is $6 + 3 = 9$. The probability of the first candy not being orange is $\frac{9}{13}$. Now, out of 12 candies, there are 8 candies left that are not orange. The probability of the second candy not being orange is $\frac{8}{12}$. Multiply these two probabilities to get the solution: $\frac{9}{13} \times \frac{8}{12} = \frac{72}{156} = \frac{24}{52} = \frac{6}{13}$

17) Choice A is correct

First calculate exponents value.

$100(3 + 0.1)^2 - 100 = 100(3.1)^2 - 100 = 100(9.61) - 100 = 961 - 100 = 861$

18) Choice B is correct

First, change the improper fractions into mixed numbers: $\frac{7}{2} = 3\frac{1}{2}$ and $\frac{30}{4} = 7\frac{1}{2}$

The integers between these two values are 4, 5, 6 and 7. So, there are 4 integers between $\frac{7}{5}$ and $\frac{30}{4}$.

19) Choice B is correct

The increase in sales tax percentage is $8.5\% - 8.0\% = 0.5\%$

0.5% of \$250 is $(0.5\%)(250) = (0.005)(250) = 1.25\$$

20) Choice A is correct

Combine like terms: $4m + 8m - 6 + 8 \rightarrow 12m + 2$

TSI Mathematics Practice Test 2

1) Choice C is correct

Let x be the number of inches representing 2.5 feet. Set up a proportion and solve for x:

$$\frac{x}{2.5} = \frac{0.15}{150} \to x = \frac{0.15 \times 2.5}{150} \to x = 0.0025 \ in$$

2) Choice D is correct

Set an equation: $\frac{3}{7}Z = 54$

Solve for Z: $\to Z = 54 \times \frac{7}{3} = 126$, then, calculate $\frac{2}{5}Z : \frac{2}{5} \times 126 = 50.4$

3) Choice B is correct

The number of pens is 14. The probability of picking a blue pen is: $\frac{8}{14} = \frac{4}{7}$

4) Choice B is correct

To answer this question, multiply 72 miles per hour to $8 \to 72 \times 8 = 576$ miles

5) Choice D is correct

The spent amount is $60, and the tip is 25%. Then: $tip = 0.25 \times 60 = \$15$

Final price = Selling price + tip → final price = $60 + $15 = $75

6) Choice D is correct

To find the smallest factor of 95, list the factors: 1, 5, 19, and 95. The smallest factor (other than 1) is 5. Of the choices listed (28, 32, 39, and 45), only 45 is a multiple of 5.

7) Choice A is correct

Adding exponents is done by calculating each exponent first and then adding and dividing:

$$\frac{4^2 + 3^2 + (-5)^2}{(9 + 10 - 11)^2} = \frac{16 + 9 + 25}{(8)^2} = \frac{50}{64} = \frac{25}{32}$$

8) Choice B is correct

Angle A and angle B are supplementary, so the sum of their angles is 180°.

Let a equal the measure of angle A, and let b equal the measure of angle B.

$a + b = 180$

The measure of angle A is 2 times the measure of angle B.

$a = 2b \to 2b + b = 180 \to 3b = 180 \to b = \frac{180}{3} = 60$

$a = 2b = 2(60) = 120$

Therefore, the measure of angle A is $120°$.

9) Choice D is correct

First calculate exponents value, then multiplying and subtracting:

$200(3 + 0.01)^2 - 200 = 200(3.01)^2 - 200 = 200(9.06) - 200 = 1,612.02$

10) Choice B is correct

Substitute -2 for x in the equation: $2(-2) + 3 = \frac{y+6}{5} \to -1 = \frac{y+6}{5} \to y + 6 = -5 \to$

$y = -5 - 6 = -11$

11) Choice D is correct

First, convert their heights from feet and inches to inches, by multiplying the number of feet by 12 and adding the inches. Tomas: 6 feet +8.5 inches. 6(12 inches) +8.5 inches= 72 inches +8.5 inches = 80.5 inches. Alex: 5 feet +3 inches. 5(12 inches)+3 inches = 60 inches + 3 inches = 63 inches

Then, subtract Alex's height from Tomas's height: $80.5 - 63 = 17.5$

12) Choice D is correct

To eliminate the decimals in this equation, multiply the numerators and denominators by 100:

$\left(\frac{0.02}{0.25}\right)\left(\frac{100}{100}\right) = \left(\frac{1.25}{x}\right)\left(\frac{100}{100}\right) \to \left(\frac{2}{25}\right) = \frac{125}{100x} \to x = \left(\frac{125}{100}\right)\left(\frac{25}{2}\right) = 15.625$

13) Choice C is correct

The first integer is m, so the second is $m + 1$, the rest are $m + 2, m + 3, m + 4, m + 5, m + 6$ and finally $m + 7$. Since n is the eight and greatest of the integers, $n = m + 7$.

Substitute $m + 7$ for n and simplify: $\frac{m+n}{3} = \frac{m+m+7}{3} = \frac{2m+7}{3}$

14) Choice C is correct

There are 6 digits in the repeating decimal (0.142857), so digit 1 would be the first, seventh, thirteenth digit and so on. To find the 68th digit, divide 68 by 6.

$68 \div 6 = 11r2$

Since the remainder is 2, that means the 68th digit is the same as the 2^{ed} digit, which is 4.

15) Choice C is correct

So far, Kylie has written $10\% + 18\% = 28\%$ of the entire homework. That means she has $100\% - 28\% = 72\%$ left to write. $72\% = \frac{72}{100} = \frac{18}{25}$

16) Choice D is correct

Let x be the number of yellow pens. Write a proportion and solve: $\frac{yellow}{blue} = \frac{2}{3} = \frac{x}{9}$

Solve the equation: $18 = 3x \rightarrow x = 6$

17) Choice B is correct

To find the decimal equivalent to $-\frac{6}{9}$, divide 6 by 9. Then:

$$-\frac{6}{9} = -0.66666\ldots = -0.\overline{6}$$

18) Choice B is correct

List the factors of 68: 1 and 68, 2 and 34, 4 and 17. There is one factor greater than 26 and less than 60.

19) Choice D is correct

First multiply 2 and -15.3. Then, calculate the result.

$-11.6 + 6.7 - 2(-15.3) = -11.6 + 6.7 + 30.6 = 25.7$

20) Choice A is correct

Let the lengths of two sides of the parallelogram be $2x\ cm$ and $3x\ cm$ respectively. Then, its perimeter $= 2(2x + 3x) = 10x$

Therefore, $10x = 40 \rightarrow x = 4$

One side $= 2(4) = 8\ cm$ and other side is: $3(4) = 12\ cm$

Effortless Math's TSI Online Center

... So Much More Online!

Effortless Math Online TSI Math Center offers a complete study program, including the following:

- ✓ Step-by-step instructions on how to prepare for the TSI Math test

- ✓ Numerous TSI Math worksheets to help you measure your math skills

- ✓ Complete list of TSI Math formulas

- ✓ Video lessons for TSI Math topics

- ✓ Full-length TSI Math practice tests

- ✓ And much more…

No Registration Required.

Visit **EffortlessMath.com/TSI** to find your online TSI Math resources.

Receive the PDF version of this book or get another FREE book!

Thank you for using our Book!

Do you LOVE this book?

Then, you can get the PDF version of this book or another book absolutely FREE!

Please email us at:

info@EffortlessMath.com

for details.

Author's Final Note

I hope you enjoyed reading this book. You've made it through the book! Great job!

First of all, thank you for purchasing this study guide. I know you could have picked any number of books to help you prepare for your TSI Math test, but you picked this book and for that I am extremely grateful.

It took me years to write this study guide for the TSI Math because I wanted to prepare a comprehensive TSI Math study guide to help test takers make the most effective use of their valuable time while preparing for the test.

After teaching and tutoring math courses for over a decade, I've gathered my personal notes and lessons to develop this study guide. It is my greatest hope that the lessons in this book could help you prepare for your test successfully.

If you have any questions, please contact me at reza@effortlessmath.com and I will be glad to assist. Your feedback will help me to greatly improve the quality of my books in the future and make this book even better. Furthermore, I expect that I have made a few minor errors somewhere in this study guide. If you think this to be the case, please let me know so I can fix the issue as soon as possible.

If you enjoyed this book and found some benefit in reading this, I'd like to hear from you and hope that you could take a quick minute to post a review on the book's Amazon page. To leave your valuable feedback, please visit: amzn.to/34VzAXY

Or scan this QR code.

I personally go over every single review, to make sure my books really are reaching out and helping students and test takers. Please help me help TSI Math test takers, by leaving a review!

I wish you all the best in your future success!

Reza Nazari

Math teacher and author

Made in the USA
Coppell, TX
17 June 2024

33614502R00090